Uniforms of the
CIVIL WAR

$1.00

February 1967

Civil War Times

ILLUSTRATED

"Drummer Boy," by Frederic Ray. (Courtesy *Civil War Times Illustrated*)

Uniforms of the
CIVIL WAR

FRANCIS A. LORD

Illustrations selected by
ARTHUR M. WISE

DOVER PUBLICATIONS, INC.
Mineola, New York

Bibliographical Note

This Dover edition, first published in 2007, is an unabridged republication
of the work published by Thomas Yoseloff, New York, 1970.

Library of Congress Cataloging-in-Publication Data

Lord Francis Alfred, 1911-
    Uniforms of the Civil War / Lord, Francis A. ; illustrations selected by
Arthur M. Wise.
        p. cm.
    "This Dover edition, first published in 2007, is an unabridged republica-
tion of the work published by Thomas Yoseloff, New York, 1970."
    Includes bibliographical references and index.
    ISBN 0-486-45420-7 (pbk.)
    1. United States—Armed Forces—Uniforms—History. I. Title.

UC483.L67 2007
973.7'8—dc22

                                                            2007000977

Manufactured in the United States of America
Dover Publications, Inc., 31 East 2nd Street, Mineola, N.Y. 11501

To
A fellow Civil War collector and valued friend
KEN MATTERN

Contents

Foreword

The uniform of American fighting men in the Civil War was essentially a legacy from previous decades, with some comparatively minor modifications. In contrast to the many significant innovations and adaptations which appeared in the "first modern war," the Federals contributed nothing basically new in the uniforming of their fighting men. Their adversaries, the Confederates, with an equal lack of constructive imagination, copied every essential from the Federals except the color of their uniforms. A notable exception, of course, was the widespread use of "butternut" which was forced on Confederates for economic rather than tactical considerations.

The 1861-1865 war was characterized by colorful uniforms. Neither side seemed to appreciate the need of a uniform that would blend well with the terrain. It remained for the Prussians, who developed their *feldgrau* in the 1870 war with France, to demonstrate the wisdom of a scientific approach to camouflage of uniforms in battle.

The average reader assumes that Federal troops wore blue uniforms and Confederate troops wore gray. This was essentially true in the case of the Federals, but much less accurate in the case of the Confederates. In Northern camps of 1861 it was hardly true at all. Few of the early Federal volunteer regiments wore blue; they wore every color of the rainbow and gray was common! The same variance in color was true for the Confederates in the early months of the war. In fact, both sides wore not only blue or gray, but also brown, green, or combinations involving black, red, or yellow.

There were thousands of units in the Federal and Confederate armies and many of them wore distinctive uniforms. Despite the multiplicity of uniforms involved, specific details on the design and color of the vast majority of them are surprisingly rare. This book depicts the basic uniform types as well as representative types of both sides.

Acknowledgments

Rear Admiral E. M. Eller
Naval historian

Norm Flayderman
New Milford, Connecticut

Colonel John H. Magruder III
Marine Corps historian

Mrs. D. C. Markham
Worthington, Massachusetts

Mike McAfee
Athens, Ohio

Jack Meyer
Urbana, Illinois

Carol Ruckdeschel
Atlanta, Georgia

James Shutt
Columbus, Ohio

H. W. Strawbridge
Diamond, Pennsylvania

Lee A. Wallace, Jr.
Arlington, Virginia

My sincere appreciation is extended to the Alderman Library of the University of Virginia for permission to use their *Uniform and Dress of the Navy of the Confederate States*.

Also I am appreciative of the assistance rendered by the Divisions of Military History and Textiles, Smithsonian Institution, for their material on preservation of military uniforms.

11

Uniforms of the
CIVIL WAR

1

Army of the United States

THE great majority of Federal troops, both Regular Army and Volunteers, wore the following uniform as prescribed in Sections 1442-1635 of *Revised Regulations for the Army of the United States 1861*.

COAT, OFFICER

All officers shall wear a frock coat of dark blue cloth, the skirt to extend from two thirds to three fourths of the distance from the top of the hip to the bend of the knee; double-breasted for all other ranks.

Major General. Two rows of buttons on the breast, nine in each row, placed by threes; the distance between each row, 5½ inches at top, and 3½ inches at bottom; stand-up collar, to rise no higher than to permit the chin to turn freely over it, to hook in front at the bottom, and slope up and backward at a 30-degree angle on each side; cuffs 2½ inches deep to go around the sleeves parallel with the lower edge, and to button with three small buttons at the under seam; pockets in the folds of the skirts, with one button at the hip, and one at the end of each pocket, making four buttons on the back and skirt of the coat, the hip button to range with the lowest buttons on the breast; collar and cuffs to be of dark blue velvet, lining of the coat black.

Brigadier General. The same as for a major general, except that there will be only eight buttons in each row on the breast, placed in pairs.

Colonel. The same as for a major general, except that there will be only seven buttons in each row on the breast, placed at equal distances; collar and cuffs of the same color and material as the coat.

Lieutenant Colonel. The same as for a colonel.

Major. The same as for a colonel.

Captain. The same as for a colonel, except that there will be only one row of nine buttons on the breast, placed at equal distances.

First Lieutenant. The same as for a captain.

Second Lieutenant. The same as for a captain.

Brevet Second Lieutenant. The same as for a captain.

Medical Cadet. The same as for a brevet second lieutenant.

Light Artillery. A round jacket of dark blue cloth, trimmed with scarlet, with the Russian shoulder knot, the prescribed insignia of rank to be worked in silver in the

Soldiers of the 4th Michigan Infantry.
Note the four-button blouses which soon
replaced the frockcoat in the field. These
four-button blouses are now extremely
rare. (Courtesy National Archives)

Federal private of light artillery. (Courtesy Smithsonian Institution)

center of the knot, may be worn on undress duty by officers of Light Artillery.

COAT, ENLISTED

All enlisted foot soldiers will wear a single-breasted frock coat of dark blue cloth, without plaits, with a skirt extending one half the distance from the top of the hip to the bend of the knee; one row of nine buttons on the breast, placed at equal distances; stand-up collar to rise no higher than to permit the chin to turn freely over it, to hook in front at the bottom and then to slope up and backward at a 30-degree angle on each side; cuffs pointed according to pattern, and to button with two small buttons at the under seams; collar and cuffs edged with a cord or welt of cloth as follows to wit:

Scarlet for artillery

Sky-blue for infantry

Yellow for engineers

Crimson for ordnance and hospital stewards

On each shoulder a metallic scale according to pattern; narrow lining for skirt of the coat of the same color and material as the coat; pockets in the folds of the skirts with one button at each hip to range with the lowest buttons on the breast; no buttons at the ends of the pockets. All enlisted men of the cavalry and light artillery shall wear a uniform jacket of dark blue cloth, with one row of 12 small buttons on the breast placed at equal distances; stand-up collar to rise no higher than to permit the chin to turn freely over it, to hook in front at the bottom, and to slope the same as the coat collar; on the collar, on each side, two blind button holes of lace, ⅜ inch wide, one small button on the button hole, lower button hole extending back 4 inches, upper button hole 3½ inches; top button and front ends of collar bound with lace ⅜ inches wide, and a strip of the same extending down the front and around the lower edge of the jacket; the back seam laced with the same, and on the cuff

a point of the same shape as that on the coat, but formed of the lace; jacket to extend to the waist, and to be lined with white flannel; two small buttons at the under seam of the cuff, as on the coat cuff; one hook and eye at the bottom of the collar; color of lace (worsted), yellow for cavalry and scarlet for light artillery.

Musicians. The same as for other enlisted men of their respective branches of service, with the addition of a facing of lace ⅜ inch wide on the front of the coat or jacket, made in the following manner; bars of ⅜ inch worsted lace placed on a line with each button 6½ inches wide at the bottom, and thence gradually expanding upward to the last button, counting from the waist up, and contracting from thence to the bottom of the collar, where it will be 6½ inches wide, with a strip of the same lace following the bars at their outer extremity—the whole presenting something of what is called the herring-bone form; the color of the lace facing to correspond with the color of the trimming of the branch of service.

Fatigue Uniform. A sack coat of dark blue flannel extending halfway down the thigh, and made loose, without sleeve or body lining, falling collar, inside pocket on the left side, 4 coat buttons down the front.

Recruit Uniform. The sack coat will be made with sleeve and body lining, the latter of flannel.

Dress Coat. The dress coat was worn by company grade officers and enlisted men and merits special discussion for that reason. Many soldiers considered the dress coat as one of their major delusions on joining the service. The dress coat was a close, tight-fitting garment, with an impressive row of brass buttons extending up to the chin, and a stiff standing collar. The sleeves were small and left little freedom of movement to the arms. The coat was worn only on formal occasions; in the early part of the war it was considered as indispensable at dress parade, inspection

Federal cavalry musician. (Courtesy Smithsonian Institution)

Federal quartermaster sergeant of cavalry.
(Courtesy Smithsonian Institution)

or review. On such occasions every button had to be buttoned, and when the mercury was in the 90's the coat was a terrible sweat-box. Not a breath of air could reach the sweltering body. On the first march the dress coats disappeared rapidly. They were thrown away to lighten knapsacks and ease aching shoulders, or were traded off to the Negroes for chickens and other eatables.

SACK COAT

Of dark blue flannel, extending half the distance down the thigh. Made loose with or without body or sleeve lining. Falling collar of double thickness cloth, edges turned under and stiched along outer edge. Four brass eagle buttons evenly spaced down front, no buttons on sleeve cuffs. Cuff split on rear seam for height of cuff, edges turned in and stitched along outer edge, also stiched along top of cuff on inside of sleeve to form a bead to outline top of cuff. All outside edges turned under and stitched. Sleeve seam at rear, edges turned inside and stitched on inside.

TROUSERS

General Officers and Officers of the Ordnance Dept. Dark blue cloth, plain without stripe, welt, or cord down the outer seam.

Officers of the General Staff and Staff Corps except the Ordnance Dept. Dark blue cloth, with a gold cord ⅛ inch in diameter, along the outer seam.

Regimental Officers. Dark blue cloth, with a welt let into the outer seam, ⅛ inch in diameter, of colors corresponding to the branch of service, viz: cavalry, yellow; artillery, scarlet; infantry, sky-blue.

Medical Cadets. Same as for officers of the General Staff, except a welt of buff cloth, instead of a gold cord.

Enlisted Men Except Companies of Light Artillery. Dark blue cloth (however, General

Order No. 108, Headquarters of the Army, December 16, 1861, authorized sky-blue as the color. Very few enlisted men wore dark blue trousers). Sergeants, with a stripe 1½ inches wide; corporals, with a stripe ½ inch wide, of worsted lace, down and over the outer seam, of the color of the respective branch of sevice; ordnance sergeants and hospital stewards, strips of crimson lace 1½ inches wide. Privates, plain without stripe or welt. Companies of artillery, equipped as light artillery, sky-blue cloth.

All trousers to be made loose, without plaits, and to spread well over the boot; to be reinforced for all enlisted mounted men.

OVERCOAT, OFFICERS

A "cloak coat" of dark blue cloth, closing by means of four frog buttons of black silk and loops of black silk cord down the breast, and at the throat by a long loop a échelle, without tassel or plate, on the left side, and a black silk frog button on the right; cord for the loops 15/100 inch in diameter; back, a single piece, slit up from the bottom, from 15 to 17 inches, according to the height of the wearer, and closing at will, by buttons, and button holes cut in a concealed flap; collar of the same color and material as the coat, rounded at the edges, and to stand or fall; when standing, to be about 5 inches high; sleeves loose, of a single piece, and round at the bottom, without cuff or slit; lining, woolen; around the front and lower border, the edges of pockets, the edges of sleeves, collar, and slit in the back a flat braid of black silk ½ inch wide; and around each frog button on the breast, a knot 2¼ inches in diameter of black silk cord, 7/100 inch in diameter; cape of the same color and material as the coat, removable at the pleasure of the wearer, and reaching to the cuff of the coat sleeve when the arm is extended; coat to extend down the leg from 6 to 8 inches below the knee, according to height. To indicate rank,

Federal private in full marching order.
(Courtesy Smithsonian Institution)

Federal infantry private in full dress.
(Courtesy Smithsonian Institution)

there will be on both sleeves near the lower edge, a knot of flat black silk braid not exceeding ⅛ inch in width, composed as follows:

General: 5 braids, double knot
Colonel: 5 braids, single knot
Lt. Colonel: 4 braids, single knot
Major: 3 braids, single knot
Captain: 2 braids, single knot
1st Lieutenant: 1 braid, single knot
2nd Lieutenant and Brevet Second Lieutenant: Plain sleeve, without knot or ornament.

OVERCOAT, ENLISTED MEN

Mounted Troops. Sky-blue cloth; stand-and-fall collar; double-breasted; cape to reach down to the cuff of the coat when the arm is extended, and to button all the way up; buttons, yellow, the same as is used by the artillery, etc., omitting the letter in the shield.

All other Enlisted Men. Sky-blue cloth; stand-up collar; single-breasted; cape to reach down to the elbows when the arm is extended, and to button all the way up; buttons, yellow, the same as is used by the artillery, etc., omitting the letter in the shield.

Infantry Overcoat. (Based on the regulations) Sky-blue kersey, burlap lining in the coat down to the waist. Skirts of coat were left unlined. Sleeves were lined with a coarse linen or burlap. Bottom of skirt was not hemmed. A standing collar, made of two layers of cloth with burlap between, and hooking from cape to chin with three hooks and eyes. A two-piece half belt was sewn in back, and was decorated with two large buttons. The cuffs on the sleeves were each 5½ inches deep and left loose so as to turn down over the hand. The coat was single breasted with five large buttons in front and six smaller buttons on the cape. The cape was unlined, but had a ⅞-inch hem at the bottom edge. The cape was approximately 14 inches long in back. The coat itself extended to half the distance of the calves of the legs. The back was 45 inches long for the average size. Back seam was split up 12 inches from the bottom edge.

Cavalry. A gutta-percha talma, or cloak extending to the knee, with long sleeves.

Talma. A talma was a long cape or cloak worn by both men and women. The term as used in the Civil War applied to the overcoat as worn by mounted men, although apparently it was sometimes used in reference to a military cloak in general.

HATS

Hat, Officers. Of the best black felt. The dimensions of medium size to be as follows: width of brim, 3¼ inches; height of crown, 6¼ inches; oval of tip, ½ inch; taper of crown, ⅜ inch. The binding to be ½ inch deep of best black ribbed silk.

Hat, Enlisted Men's. Of black felt, same shape and size as for officers with double row of stitching, instead of binding, around the edge. To agree in quality with the pattern deposited in the clothing arsenal.

Hat, Medical Cadets. Will wear a forage cap according to pattern.

Hat Trimmings, General Officers. Gold cord, with acorn-shaped ends. The brim of the hat looped up on the right side, and fastened with an eagle attached to the side of the hat; three black ostrich feathers on the left side; a gold embroidered wreath in front, on black velvet ground, encircling the letters U.S. in silver, old English characters.

Officers of the Adjutant General's, Inspector-General's, Quartermaster's, Subsistence, Medical and Pay Department and the Judge Advocate, Above the Rank of Captain. The same as for general officers, except the cord, which will be black silk and gold.

Same Departments, Below the Rank of Field Officers. The same as for field officers, except that there will be but two feathers.

Officers of the Corps of Engineers. The

Federal private in overcoat. (Courtesy
Smithsonian Institution)

same as for the General Staff, except the ornament in front, which will be a gold embroidered wreath of laurel and palm, encircling a silver-turreted castle on black velvet ground.

OFFICERS OF THE TOPOGRAPHICAL ENGINEERS

The same as for the General Staff, except the ornament in front which will be a gold-embroidered wreath of oak leaves, encircling a gold-embroidered shield, on black velvet ground.

Officers of the Ordnance Dept. The same as for the General Staff, except the ornament in front, which will be a gold-embroidered shell and flame, on black velvet ground.

Officers of Cavalry. The same as for the General Staff, except the ornament in front, which will be two gold embroidered sabers, crossed, edges upward, on black velvet ground, with the number of the regiment in silver in the upper angle.

Officers of Artillery. The same as for the General Staff except the ornament in front which will be gold-embroidered cross cannon, on black velvet ground, with the number of the regiment in silver at the intersection of the cross cannon.

Officers of Infantry. The same as for artillery, except the ornament in front, which will be a gold-embroidered bugle, on black velvet ground, with the number of the regiment in silver within the bend.

Enlisted Men, except Companies of Light Artillery. The same as for officers of the respective corps, except that there will be but one feather, the cord will be worsted, of the same color as that of the facing of the branch of service, 3/16 inch in diameter, running three times through a slide of the same material, and terminating with two tassels, not less than 2 inches long, on the side of the hat opposite the feather. The insignia of branch of service, in brass, in front of the hat, cor-responding with those prescribed for officers, with the number of regiment, ⅝ inch long, in brass, and letter of company, 1 inch, in drass, arranged over insignia.

Hospital Stewards. The cord will be of buff and green mixed. The wreath in front of brass, with the letters U.S. in Roman, of white metal. Brim to be looped up to side of hat with a brass eagle, having a hook attached to the bottom to secure the brim—on the right side for mounted men and left side for foot men. The feathers to be worn on the side opposite the loop. All the trimmings of the hat are to be made so that they can be detached; but the eagle, badge of branch of service, and letter of company, are to be always worn.

Companies of Artillery, Equipped as Light Artillery. The old pattern uniform cap, with red horsehair plume, cord and tassel.

Light Artillery Uniform Hat. Lt. Philip S. Chase, Battery F, 1st Rhode Island Light Artillery, believed that it was very rare when a volunteer battery secured the full regulation light artillery uniform which included the horeshair plume, the cord over the shoulders, the rosette on the breast and tassels. Lt. Chase remarked after the war that he "never happened to see another during my term of service, and never saw ours but once after we left North Carolina."

Officers of the General Staff and Staff Corps. May wear, at their option, a light French chapeau, either stiff crown or flat, according to the pattern deposited in the Adjutant General's office. Officers below the rank of field officers to wear but two feathers.

Forage Caps. For fatigue purposes, forage caps, of pattern in Quartermaster General's Office: dark blue cloth, with a welt of the same around the crown, and yellow metal letters in front to designate companies. (Often however, enlisted men wore regimental numbers, badge of branch of service, or corps badges.) Commissioned officers could wear forage caps of the same pattern, with the dis-

Federal hospital steward. (Courtesy Smithsonian Institution)

Federal infantry corporal, full dress, rear
view. (Courtesy Smithsonian Institution)

Burnside and staff—a month before Fredericksburg. Note the tall hats worn by imitators of Burnside. (Courtesy Library of Congress)

tinctive ornament of the branch of service and regiment in front. (Officers also wore corps badges after their authorization in 1863.)

Some officers and many soldiers wore the forage cap copied after the French kepi. The "McClellan cap" was a fairly faithful copy of the French kepi, but the "bummers cap" was as "shapeless as a feed bag" and not attractive at all. It had a leather visor which curled up when dry and drooped when wet. Nevertheless, this ungainly and unsightly headgear was roomy enough in the top for a wet sponge, green leaves, or a handkerchief.

Light Artillery Shako. In the catalogue of Schuyler, Hartley and Graham the ornaments of this shako differ from those shown in the photograph from the Smithsonian Institution. The latter photograph dates from early in the war, probably 1862, while the catalogue was printed in 1864. This may explain the following differences: In the catalogue illustration the eagle resembles the eagle on the Hardee hat and the plume holder is a plain cup. But in the Smithsonian photograph the eagle resembles those worn in the 1830's as does the plume holder. It is probable, therefore, that the early shakos, i.e.,

1861-1862, were trimmed with leftover 1830 insignia, while the later shakos, i.e., 1864, used plainer and more recent insignia, such as the Hardee eagle.

CRAVAT OR STOCK

Officers. Black. When a cravat was worn, the tie was not to be visible at the opening of the collar.

Enlisted Men. Black leather, according to pattern. Early in the war soldiers had to wear these leather collars to force them to hold their heads erect. These "dog collars," as the men dubbed them, were pieces of stiff upper leather, about 2 inches wide in the middle and tapering to 1 inch at the ends, which were fastened by buckles. Like the havelocks, these leather collars soon disappeared and are very rare today.

SASH

General Officers. Buff, net, with silk bullion fringe ends; sash to go twice around the waist, and to tie behind the left hip, pendant part not to extend more than 18 inches below the tie.

Officers of Adjutant-General's, Inspector-General's, Quartermaster's and Subsistence Department, Corps of Engineers, Topographical Engineers, Ordnance, Artillery, Infantry, Cavalry, and the Judge Advocate of the Army. Crimson silk net.

Officers of the Medical Department. Medium or emerald green silk net, with silk bullon fringe ends; to go around the waist and tie as for general officers.

Sergeant Majors, Quartermaster Sergeants, Ordnance Sergeants, Hospital Stewards, First Sergeants, Principal or Chief Musicians, and Chief Buglers. Red worsted sash, with worsted bullion fringe ends; to go twice around the waist, and to tie behind the left hip, pendant part not to extend more than 18 inches below the tie.

The sash will be worn over the coat on all occasions of duty of every description, except stable and fatigue. The sash will be worn, by "Officers of the Day," across the body, scarf fashion, from the right shoulder to the left side, instead of around the waist, tying behind the left hip as prescribed.

BOOTS AND SHOES

Officers. Ankle or Jefferson.

Enlisted Men of Cavalry and Light Artillery. Ankle and Jefferson, rights and lefts, according to pattern.

Enlisted Men of Artillery, Infantry, Engineers, Ordnance. Jefferson, rights and lefts, according to pattern.

Military Storekeeper. A citizen's frockcoat of blue cloth, with buttons of the branch or service to which attached; round black hat; trousers and vest, plain white or dark blue; cravat or stock, black.

Band Members. Bandsmen will wear the uniform of the regiment or branch of service to which they belong. The commanding officer may, at the expense of the branch of service, sanctioned by the Council of Administration, make such additions in ornaments as he may judge proper.

Signal Officer. By General Order No. 32, U.S. War Dept. June 15, 1861, the uniform and dress were to be that of a major of the General Staff.

SHOULDER STRAPS

Lieut.-General Commanding the Army. Dark blue cloth, $1\frac{3}{8}$ inches wide by 4 inches long; bordered with an embroidery of gold $\frac{1}{4}$ inch wide; three silver-embroidered stars of five rays one star on the center of the strap, and one on each side equidistant between the center and the outer edge of the strap; the center star to be the largest.

Major General. The same as for the Lieut. General Commanding the Army, except that

Federal major general (General George B.
McClellan). (Courtesy National Archives)

there were two stars instead of three; the center of each star being 1 inch from the outer edge of the gold embroidery on the ends of the strap; both stars were of the same size.

Brigadier General. The same as for a major general, except that there was one star instead of two; the center of the star being equidistant from the outer edge of the embroidery on the ends of the strap.

Colonel. The same size as for a major general, and bordered in like manner with an embroidery of gold; a silver-embroidered spread eagle on the center of the strap, 2 inches between the tips of the wings, having

in the right talon an olive branch, and in the left a bundle of arrows; an escutcheon on the breast, as represented in the arms of the United States; cloth of the strap as follows: for the *General Staff and Staff Corps*—dark blue; *Artillery*—scarlet; *Infantry*—light or sky blue; *Cavalry*—yellow.

Lieutenant Colonel. The same as for a colonel, according to branch of service, omitting the eagle and substituting a silver-embroidered leaf at each end, each leaf extending ⅞ of an inch from the end border of the strap.

Major. The same as for a colonel according to branch of service, omitting the eagle, and

Federal band in dress uniform. (Courtesy Library of Congress)

Federal bandsmen in dress uniform. (Courtesy Library of Congress)

substituting a gold-embroidered leaf at each end, each leaf extending ⅞ of an inch from the end border of the strap.

Captain. The same as for a colonel, according to branch of service, omitting the eagle and substituting at each end two gold-embroidered bars of the same width as the border, placed parallel to the ends of the strap; the distance between them and from the border equal to the width of the border.

First Lieutenant. The same as for a colonel, according to branch of service, omitting the eagle, and substituting at each end one gold-embroidered bar of the same width as the border, placed parallel to the ends of the strap, at a distance from the border equal to its width.

Second Lieutenant. The same as for a colonel, according to branch of service, omitting the eagle.

Brevet Second Lieutenant. The same as for a second lieutenant.

Medical Cadet. A strip of gold lace 3 inches long, ½ inch wide placed in the middle of a strap of green cloth 3¾ inches long by 1¼ inches wide.

The shoulder strap was worn whenever the epaulette was not.

Miniature insignia of rank were worn by some officers in lieu of the conspicuous shoulder straps. By General Orders No. 286, November 22, 1864, the War Department permitted officers in the field to dispense with shoulder straps, but they had to continue to wear their rank designation.

At times officers were strongly advised to

Bandsmen of the 4th Michigan Infantry.
(Courtesy The National Archives)

remove their shoulder straps in combat to make their wearers less conspicuous to an ever vigilant enemy.

NOTES ON THE REGULATION UNIFORM

In addition to the modifications in use of individual uniform items indicated above, the following adaptations and explanations are essential to a description of the regulation uniform.

Uniform of General Officers
Despite the explicit detail of the Army Regulations, Federal generals showed their individuality in dress. While it is true that men like McClellan, Hooker, and Hancock strictly adhered to the Regulations in their wearing of the uniform, many other officers departed widely from the Regulations in their uniforms.

Grant usually wore a private's blouse; his rank as lieutenant general was only indicated by his shoulder straps. Irvin McDowell, the hapless commander at both battles of Bull Run, wore a pith hat or helmet to protect him from the rays of the sun. In August

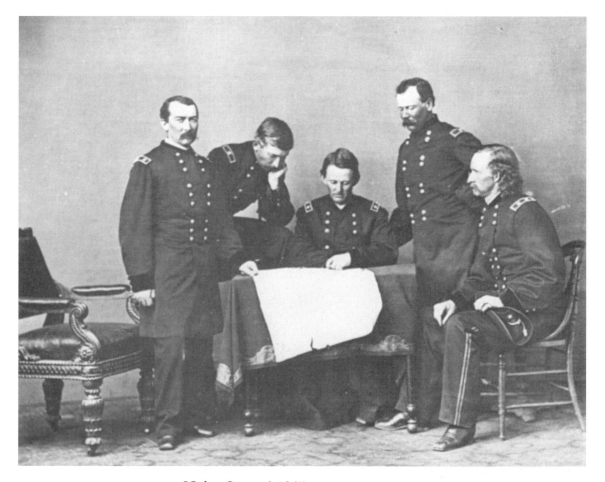

Major General Philip H. Sheridan and his commanders. (Courtesy The National Archives)

Service Chevron—One Enlistment.

Service Chevrons—Two Enlistments.

CORPORAL'S Chevrons.

SERGEANT'S Chevrons.

1st SERGEANT.

Ordnance SERGEANT.

QUARTERMASTER'S SERGEANT.

SERGEANT-MAJOR.

Civil War chevrons.

36

Young Federal in overcoat. (Courtesy The
Cooper Union Museum, New York)

Group of officers at Artillery Headquarters, Culpeper, Va., Sept. 1863. (Courtesy Library of Congress)

1862, this hat, which "looked like an inverted washbowl," aroused much unfavorable comment among his troops. Burnside, always popular with his men, was described by one of them (just before Antietam) as follows:

He was dressed so as to be almost unrecognizable as a general officer; wore a rough blouse on the collar of which a close look revealed two much-battered and faded stars, indicating his rank of major general. He wore a black "Slouch" hat, the brim well down over his face.

Dress Uniform

The dress uniform was not worn by either officer or men to any extent once they arrived at the front. We get an erroneous opinion of the extensive use of the dress uniform because many soldiers and officers had their pictures taken in them either before leaving the state for the war, or while home on furlough or after discharge.

Veteran troops, often unfairly, tended to sneer at well-uniformed troops.

A slur upon a soldier because he was enabled and ordered to dress somewhat like a gentleman, should never come from a comrade, even if the latter must lie in mud with only a shelter tent to cover him. Some troops must perform such service, and the best troops were needed (in such concentration areas as Washington or Richmond) as well as at the front. Further, no regiment or number of regiments monopolized this preferred duty. . . . Neat uniforms, polished brasses, and white gloves were necessary in Washington. In the trenches around Petersburg, or on the march to the sea, they would have been an absurdity. (Color Sergeant Francis H. Buffum, 14th New Hampshire Infantry)

Once in the field, baggage was generally reduced to a minimum, and this included all surplus clothing. Trunks and boxes were sent home and dress uniforms were hung up in closets. These uniforms looked exceedingly nice on dress parade or review, but were out of place on a forced march or in battle.

Fatigue Uniform

Except for cavalry and artillery units, there was no "fatigue uniform" as such during the Civil War. Soldiers performed manual labor, such as digging intrenchments and policing up the camp area, in their uniforms. The

Custer (left) as Second Lieutenant and brother officers. Photo by James F. Gibson. (Courtesy Library of Congress)

Upper group: The Civil War soldier as
he really looked and marched.

Lower group: "Right shoulder shift"—col-
umns of fours—The 22nd New York on the
road. (Courtesy *Review of Reviews*)

amount of such manual labor varied with units and their military assignments. Certainly one of the most unique units of the war was a Chicago battalion, consisting of 214 men, and commanded by a Captain J. W. Wilson. This unit, called "The Illinois Bridge, Breastwork and Fortification Fusileers," was composed of:

- 120 carpenters
- 70 railroad-track men
- 7 railroad and bridge blacksmiths
- 6 boat builders
- 2 engineers
- 9 locomotive builders

Uniforms after campaigning

At the end of an arduous campaign, a regiment no longer looked finely clothed. Rather, the visitor saw ragged, dusty, broken-up companies. There were slouch hats, straw hats, caps of nearly every hue and pattern; trousers in like condition and scorched in many instances to the knee. Some men would be without shoes, and many with no socks at all. Such was the appearance of the 22nd Massachusetts Infantry September 2, 1862, at the end of the Peninsular Campaign. It had been in service exactly one year. And the appearance of this regiment was similar to most regiments—east or west—after their first few months of active campaigning.

OVERCOAT

Volunteers in the early months of the war wore overcoats of widely varying hues and quality. Overcoats issued to the 5th Massachusetts Volunteer Militia were of "very poor grade of shoddy" and black in color. Not only was the cloth poor in quality, it would not hold the coloring put into it. The soldier on guard in the rain soon found that the color of his overcoat ran, coloring his clothing and body. Resentment grew among the men, and as they marched down State Street in Boston on their way to the transport ship,

they decided to throw their overcoats into the street. Accordingly, the quartermaster called in the overcoats and the men marched off without them. The home folks got into the controversy and soon the Governor received a letter from Medford, November 14, 1862:

"Why don't you see that Drunken Bill Schouler (Adjutant General of Massachusetts) sends the Fifth Regiment their overcoats."

[Signed]
"Smith"

Each member of the 40th New York Infantry was issued a heavy black overcoat, trimmed and lined with red flannel. This overcoat was later turned in for the light blue regulation overcoat.

Some officers purchased special overcoats. For example, the quartermaster of the 149th New York Infantry had a "new-fangled" tent and overcoat combined.

But no matter what type of overcoat the men wore, they were extremely careless about their overcoats and lost or sold them at the first opportunity.

After Fredericksburg, when money was scarce and tobacco practically unavailable from the sutler, many men traded their overcoats for the tobacco they craved. Often Federals even traded their overcoats to Confederate soldiers for tobacco. However, the Confederates didn't wear the overcoats thus acquired, but sold them to eager civilians in Richmond for $100 each.

If the men did not sell their overcoats by the time spring came around, they threw them away on the first long march in warm weather. Grant noted that on the march toward the Wilderness in the Spring of 1864, his men threw away large numbers of overcoats. The General had never witnessed such wastage at any time previously in his military career.

Federal army poncho. (Courtesy Smithsonian Institution)

PONCHO

One of the most desirable and well-made items of uniform was the poncho. It was made of rubber cloth, 6 feet long, 4 feet wide, with a slit 18 inches in length, running crosswise in the center. At night the soldier spread it on the ground under his woolen blankets, or used it as a tent over him.

He wore it in rainy weather by thrusting his head through the slit, allowing the poncho to fall loosely around his body from the shoulders—thus covering the soldier as a mantle. With the "gum" side outward, the poncho gave excellent protection from the rain.

Officially called poncho, this word had no meaning to the soldier, who always called it the "gum blanket."

HEADGEAR

In 1858 the War Department adopted a dress hat known commonly as the "Jeff Davis" hat after Jefferson Davis who was Secretary of War at the time. Sometimes the hat was called the "Hardee" hat after Major William J. Hardee, 2nd United States Cavalry. This crack unit was one of the first regiments to wear the new dress hat. This headgear was very ornate. Looped up on the side with a brass eagle ornament, it also had a cord whose color designated the branch of service, and from one to three ostrich feathers, depending on the rank of the wearer. The hat, uncomfortable and gaudy in appearance, was unpopular with most soldiers. A notable exception was the famous Iron Brigade who wore

Chapeaux, Hats, and Caps.

U. S. A. Regulation Chapeau.

U. S. Felt Hat.

Fatigue Cap, with Oiled
Silk Cover.

Fatigue Cap, with Gold,
or Silk Braid.

Burnside Pattern Felt Hat.

Federal headgear.

Federal cap insignia. (Courtesy Mike Mc-Afee)

theirs proudly as a special mark of distinction. More rarely worn than the Jeff Davis head-gear was the "Burnside Pattern Felt Hat," which was a modified form of the Jeff Davis hat.

So far as the Jeff Davis hat was concerned, the average soldier "lost" his at the first opportunity. Men of the 111th Pennsylvania Infantry were among many units issued the hat at their muster in. When the train carrying the regiment halted on a bridge spanning the Shenandoah River, the men saluted the historic stream by pitching their hated hats into the river. From that day on they wore the regulation forage caps.

A soldier in the 13th Massachusetts Infantry found the Jeff Davis hat neither useful nor ornamental. He described his hat as "made of black felt, high-crowned, with a wide rim turned up on one site, and fastened to the crown by a brass shield representing an eagle with extended wings, apparently screaming with holy horror." The men lined their hats with newspaper but still the hated hats came down over their eyes. Soon the hats of the 13th Massachusetts began to disappear mysteriously. Other regiments had similar experiences and it was not long before the Jeff Davis hat was worn only by newly enlisted soldiers.

The forage cap was the commonly worn headgear in the East, while the hat was more popular with Western troops. But in addition to the Jeff Davis hat worn by new troops and the Iron Brigade, a few Eastern units preferred hats. The 16th New York Infantry wore straw hats on the Peninsula in 1862, and the 3rd New Hampshire Infantry wore helmets in the early months of service. This helmet was similar in appearance to the tropical pith helmet of today.

The regulation or "Jeff Davis" hat was sharply criticized. An officer's letter, printed in the *Army and Navy Journal* for September 12, 1863, called attention to the regulation hat. In scathing terms the officer pointed out that the ostrich feather was a useless expense and a "barbarous imitation of the tatooed Indian." (!) The officer suggested that the forage cap be used exclusively in the army, pointing out that the hat helped deserters because it so closely resembled the civilian hat of the day. However, even the forage cap was unsatisfactory; it was a waste of cloth. The cap was too baggy and blew off the head too easily. This officer concluded that the felt hat as worn by the Confederates was the best of all military headgear of the opposing armies. Best of all, said the officer, was the British Army cap because it was stiff and had a square visor.

General Henry Prince of the 2nd Division, 3rd Corps, and staff. Photo by T. H. O'Sullivan. (Courtesy Library of Congress)

Artwork showing group of enlisted men. U.S. Signal Corps. (Courtesy The National Archives)

HAVELOCK

This "foreign contraption" derived its name from the English general who distinguished himself in the 1857 war in India where they were first worn. The havelock was a white linen covering for the cap and neck of the soldier in hot weather. American soldiers never adopted the havelock and it soon passed out of use except as patches for cleaning muskets! However, in early 1861 relatives and friends made them by the thousands for their soldiers. Frequently soldiers were provided with two each; a Connecticut company received six per man!

Most havelocks were made large enough to cover the neck and shoulders and thereby deprived the wearer of any air he might otherwise have enjoyed. The motive which prompted the States to supply them was a good one. Equally good was the action of men of the 13th Massachusetts Infantry who transferred them at once "to the plebeian uses of dishcloth or a coffee-strainer."

Like several other innovations in uniform items, the havelock soon became an object

Regiment of Sherman veterans, 21st Michigan Infantry. U.S. Signal Corps, Brady Collection. (Courtesy The National Archives)

47

of ridicule to its wearers. Widely read at the time were the scathing comments of the famous American humorist, Orpheus C. Kerr, who said of the havelocks that the soldiers at first took them to be shirts! Kerr wrote that if the women of America could manage to get a little less linen in the collars of the havelocks and a little more into the other pants of the "graceful garmint," there would be fewer colds in the army. "The havelocks . . . are very roomy . . . " A soldier put one on at night when he went on sentry duty and looked like "a broomstick in a pillow case"—he encountered an officer who roared at him "to go to his tent and take off that nightgown."

SHOULDER SCALES

Made of stamped brass and attached to the coat by means of a wing stud sewed to the coat on top of the shoulder next to the collar. The stud fitted through a T-slat on the scale and turned 90 degrees to prevent the scale from falling off. Shoulder scales were worn by light-artillerymen, cavalrymen, NCO's, musicians, and infantry privates. But most veterans soon threw their "scales" away as being useless and conspicuous. However, early volunteers did wear them in substantial numbers. The theoretical value of shoulder scales was to ward off saber cuts across the shoulders.

NECKERCHIEF

This item was very rarely worn during the Civil War; it became popular only in the postwar period during Indian campaigning in the West. However, it was worn during the war by a few individuals. For example, E. F. Ware of Co. E, 1st Iowa Infantry, proudly wore his handkerchief as a necktie and a neckerchief. On the march he put the ends around his hat and let it hang down like a havelock. This kept the sun from the back of his neck and prevented sunstroke. This "neckerchief" was a large square, red-bordered, cotton handkerchief with a large blue steamboat plying up a picturesque yellow river in the center. Ware found the handkerchief invaluable and it cost him only fifty cents in Boonville, Missouri, in 1861.

SHOES

Army shoes, called "brogans" or "whangs," were large, heavy, and roomy. At first, the recruits preferred civilian patent leather shoes or boots, but soon learned that army shoes were best for long marches. Quality varied and often paper and wood were substituted for leather.

In retrospect, veterans agreed with the statement of the historian of the 40th New York infantry who maintained that the army brogan was not elegant but excellent for marching. He asserted he never knew of a comrade who suffered from sore feet caused by the army shoe. "The wide heel and broad sole of the army brogan promote ease and comfort in marching." However, most veterans soaped their socks prior to a long march. This had the effect of reducing most of the friction caused by walking, and materially reduced foot soreness and blistering.

Many soldiers testified that, while boots *looked* good, they were useless on long marches. As a soldier of the 149th New York Infantry moaned: "Great Scott! Why will a shoemaker never learn to make a pair of boots easy?" In despair, he put on a pair of army shoes and the remainder of his march was much more comfortable. Actually, the footwear called "Jefferson boots" were shoes which extended two inches above the ankle joint. This "boot" was similar to the "ankle boot" of the period except that the "ankle boot" had several eyelets for lacing. "Jefferson boots" had low heels and were tied with a single thong.

As with other items of clothing, shoes were

President Lincoln and General George B. McClellan in the General's tent. Photo by Alex Gardner. (Courtesy Library of Congress)

Captain George E. Custer and General Alfred Pleasonton on horseback, Falmouth, Va., 1863. Photo by T. O'Sullivan. (Courtesy Library of Congress)

often in short supply due to faulty distribution. For example, as winter approached, the 10th Massachusetts Infantry suffered from a lack of shoes, and a neighboring regiment had about a hundred men marching without shoes. Where the "number seven" shoe was unobtainable, the quartermasters had issued the "number eight" shoe. But the men refused to take a shoe larger than the proper size for them.

BUTTONS

In addition to the buttons prescribed by regulations, many regiments wore buttons with their state seals on them. Rubber buttons, patented by Goodyear in 1851, were worn by Berdan's sharpshooters. These rubber buttons did not glisten in the sun as did the regulation brass buttons. A three-string lyre insignia was used on buttons worn by some musicians.

BELT BUCKLES

The regulation buckle was oval in shape with U.S. in block letters in the center of the buckle. Some Federal regiments wore their state letters or militia designation in lieu of the regulation U.S. The more commonly worn were: S.N.Y. (State of New York), O.V.M. (Ohio Volunteer Militia), V.M.M. (Volunteer Maine Militia), etc. Noncommissioned officers, musicians, and cavalrymen wore buckles similar to that worn by commissioned officers.

2

U. S. Militia—Zouaves—Chasseurs

MILITIA

THE militia regiments from 1850 to 1861 generally wore the same uniform. In fact, it closely resembled the 1851 regulation uniform of the Regular Army. For example, the uniform of Connecticut militia consisted of a frockcoat, trousers, and leather shako—all of dark blue cloth. Branches of service were shown by a system of colored pompoms. Usually the state coat of arms was also worn on the leather shako.

The earliest units to leave for the front were the militia regiments which responded to Lincoln's April 15th call for 75,000 men. These regiments reported at their armories in the old uniforms, many dating back to the Mexican War or even earlier. Since these militia regiments were brought up to full war strength only a few days before leaving their states for the front, many of the new militiamen were without uniforms at all.

In these early months of the war, several Federal regiments were attired in militia gray uniforms. Among them were: 1st Massachusetts Infantry, 3rd New York Infantry, 1st Vermont Infantry, 1st Iowa Infantry, as well as units from Indiana, Maine, Nebraska, Kansas, and Wisconsin.

Blue uniforms were worn by: 13th Massachusetts Infantry, 22nd Pennsylvania Infantry, as well as several Vermont and New York regiments, including the "American Guard" (71st New York Infantry)

Many regiments did wear gray uniforms. It seemed somewhat an accident that the South adopted the gray, since it had been worn by Northern militia units for many years prior to the war.

Most of the early Federal volunteers joined these militia units which had been in existence for years prior to the war. Accordingly, these early volunteers wore the uniforms of the old militia regiments in which they enlisted. However, despite frantic efforts of the state quartermasters, many of these early volunteers were still in civilian clothes after several weeks in camp. The uniforms worn by their more fortunate comrades mingled with every variety of costume, giving a curiously grotesque effect to the early regimental drill formation.

The early regiments of foreign volunteers generally confined their distinction in dress to special headgear and emblems on their regimental flags.

VERMONT

The 1st Vermont Infantry wore a gray uniform and gray overcoat. Two companies wore a blue uniform. Each man wore a hemlock sprig in his hat.

Group of officers of the Horse Artillery near Fair Oak, Va., May 1862. Photo by James F. Gibson. (Courtesy Library of Congress)

NEW HAMPSHIRE

The 2nd New Hampshire Infantry wore a gray uniform, including a "spike-tail" coat banded with red cord and a jaunty forage cap.

RHODE ISLAND

The 1st Rhode Island Infantry wore a mixed uniform consisting of the regulation hat, gray trousers, and the famous "Burnside blouse," a loose-fitting blue blouse.

The 2nd Rhode Island Infantry in June 1861 was issued its uniform consisting of the "Burnside" (also called "Rhode Island")

blouse, gray pants, and regulation hat. This blouse was a pleated affair, whose length was a compromise between the short jacket and the dress frockcoat.

MASSACHUSETTS

The 1st Battalion of Rifles of Massachusetts in April 1861 wore a dark green uniform, trimmed with light green.

The Boston Rifle Company, armed with the Whitney rifle and saber bayonet, on May 12, 1861, wore: light blue pants, red shirt, dark gray overcoat, and fatigue cap.

Independent Corps of Cadets, from 1861

A Union volunteer of 1861. (Courtesy Library of Congress)

to 1864, wore a gray uniform trimmed with red, leather shako with a red pompom decorated with a red and white rosette, or, on dress occasions, a black chapeau with red plume. This uniform was worn mainly in the state, but a blue uniform took its place in the field.

CONNECTICUT

In 1859 the "New Haven Grays" wore blue frock coats with red shoulder knots and blue pants, all richly finished in gilt and braid, a very striking and handsome uniform."

Another early regiment, the 4th Connecticut Infantry, in 1861, writhed under very heavy uniforms which were made of the thickest sort of gray woolen—"made, one would have thought, especially for midwinter wear in Greenland." There were heavy gray felt hats to match. There were no blouses, but short coats, without skirts; "the pants of so generous girth that if any hero should retreat, he had a good hiding place for his knapsack belongings."

Some of the trousers were three inches too long, others nearly that much too short. Coats were too big. There were no vests. The shirts were coarse, heavy gray flannel.

54

NEW YORK

7th New York Infantry

This famous militia unit adopted the various items of its uniform by stages and at different times. In 1849 it adopted white leather belts and the box knapsack. The next year it adopted an overcoat of sky-blue army kersey, single-breasted, with cape, and provided with seven large state buttons. Shortly thereafter (1853) the regiment was equipped with the militia shako hat.

In December 1862, this regiment wore a gray fatigue jacket cap, gray trousers, light-blue overcoat, black waist belt, knapsack of black straps (replacing the old white straps of 1861), and a haversack.

Major General Benjamin F. Butler, Massachusetts Militia. (Courtesy Library of Congress)

The "Rhode Island blouse." Lt. James H. Chapel, 1st Rhode Island Infantry. U.S. Signal Corps photo, Brady Collection. (Courtesy The National Archives)

13th New York Infantry

Uniforms worn by this unit at First Bull Run were "hastily ordered and hastily made." Apparently these uniforms were made by a greedy contractor, who slighted quality in his product, which was far below government specifications. The uniforms were of a dull gray shoddy material and fitted the men badly. Soon these uniforms, dubbed the "Penitentiary Uniforms," were worn out. The men looked like a ragged mob—dressed only in shirts and drawers, many with no shoes or stockings. The seats of the baggy trousers were gone even though the men attempted to repair them by gathering the tattered edges together and binding them with a few straws as a farmer would fasten the opening of a grain bag.

Group of 4th Michigan Infantry. U.S. Signal Corps, Brady Collection. (Courtesy The National Archives)

Frockcoat and four-button blouse—Federal officer and private. U.S. Signal Corps photo, Brady Collection. (Courtesy The National Archives)

Militia uniforms, 7th New York Infantry.
U.S. Signal Corps photo, Brady Collection.
(Courtesy The National Archives)

20th New York Infantry

The only uniform worn by this regiment for several weeks after muster in April 1861, was a soft, light-colored Kossuth hat, and a leather collar about two inches high. Otherwise, the uniform was regulation.

"Union Grays" (22nd New York Infantry)

This militia regiment wore a single-breasted frockcoat, cut in the French style, made of gray cloth, with red collar and cuffs, trimmed with white piping. The trousers also were gray, with a red stripe, edged with white piping down the sides. The cap was gray, with red band and top, each edged with white

piping. Also worn were yellow leather leggings.

31st New York Infantry

This regiment had several Polish companies. The men wore the Polish quadrangular caps of red and white.

"Garibaldi Guard" (39th New York Infantry)

This regiment, commanded by Colonel Fred George D'Utassy, numbered 830 officers and men. Its ten companies comprised the following nationalities:

French, 1 company
Italian, 1 company

Band in dress uniform. (Courtesy Library of Congress)

Federal band. (Courtesy The National Archives)

Swiss, 1 company
Spanish, 1 company
German, 3 companies
Hungarian, 3 companies

This regiment wore a uniform which was a copy of the famed Bersaglieri of Italy. The uniform consisted of a red flannel shirt with a broad collar, dark blue trousers, black leather leggings, and a soft felt hat with a cock feather.

"Mozart Regiment" (40th New York Infantry)

Since many men in this regiment were from Massachusetts, the men left for the front wearing the Massachusetts gray uni-forms consisting of a double-breasted frock-coat. But later these uniforms were sent back to Massachusetts. However, it was rumored that they never reached Massachusetts. They were sold to secondhand clothing dealers in New York City.

"Schwarzer Jaeger" (54th New York Infantry)

This regiment, consisting exclusively of Germans, many of whom had seen service in their native land, was recruited in 1861 in New York City as the "Schwarzer Jaeger" ("Black Rifles"). They were uniformed in black and silver like the regiment they were named after ("Lutzow's Schwarzer Jaeger") and carried the Stars and Stripes.

Mexican War uniforms used in 1861. Drummer boys of the 8th New York National Guard. (Courtesy Library of Congress)

Militia bandsmen, Drum Corps, 8th New York State Militia, Arlington, Va., June 1861. (Courtesy Library of Congress)

Federal drummer boy. U.S. Signal Corps photo, Brady Collection. (Courtesy The National Archives)

"Gardes Lafayette" (55th New York Infantry)

Wore a light blue coat with black trimming on the sleeves, and a red cap.

79th N.Y. "Highlanders" (79th New York Infantry)

Nucleus of this regiment was the "Highland Guard," a crack New York City militia battalion, composed of Scots, or men of Scottish ancestry. They wore the kilt as their dress uniform. But for undress or fatigue, they wore a blue jacket with red facings, and trousers of Cameronian tartan. This is the uniform the Highlanders—now a full regiment—wore to the front in 1861. In August 1861, this regiment still wore the blue jacket with red facings, but the regulation uniform for the rest of their outfit. Still later, when the jackets had worn out, the men were uniformed like other Federal infantry regiments.

The kilts were worn on dress parade in Washington by the 79th, but when the regiment crossed over into Virginia, both the kilts and plaid trousers were left behind and the regulation blue worn. The only officer to wear kilts into Virginia was so roundly guyed he left them behind as the regiment neared the Bull Run battle.

128th New York Infantry

Soldiers of this regiment complained of the "sickly blue" as the worst possible color possible for a uniform. As a member of the regiment said: "I guess the Government had more cloth than color." Another said that the Government had only one kettle of dye for its uniforms. "The officers' clothes were dipped first, then the privates' coats, and last the pantaloons."

PENNSYLVANIA

"Bucktails" (13th Pennsylvania Reserves)

According to the regimental history, James Landregan of the "McKean County Rifles" saw a deer's hide hanging outside a butcher's shop in Smethport, Pennsylvania, where the men were quartered before leaving the state. Landregan crossed the street, pulled out his penknife, cut off the tail, and stuck it in his cap. Upon his return to headquarters, Colonel Thomas L. Kane noticed the soldier's headgear and announced that the unit he was recruiting would be known as "Bucktails."

An interesting sequel was the attempt of the 88th Pennsylvania Infantry to imitate the "Bucktails" with squirrel tails! When members of Company "B" of the 88th Regiment were on guard duty, they found themselves in woods heavily infested with squirrels. The men soon began to save the tails of squirrels they shot. Soon all members of the company had their "bushes" and each man fastened one to his cap in imitation of Colonel Kane's famous "Bucktail" regiment. The officers of Company "B" were proud of the unique appearance of their men adorned with this new headgear, and decided to give the colonel a pleasant surprise by appearing at the first dress parade with their new plumage. But when Company "B" took its place in line at "Retreat," there was too sharp a contrast between"B" and all other companies of the regiment. The Colonel was greatly displeased, however, and ordered the company commander to have the squirrel tails removed from the uniform at once.

INDIANA

Of the first six regiments from Indiana in early 1861, only the one commanded by Colonel Lew Wallace had a uniform of its own design. The other five regiments let out bids in the state for their uniforms. The details for these uniforms are sketchy, but apparently they consisted of a Hardee-pattern hat, gray or blue jackets and trousers.

ZOUAVES

The most popular of all uniforms in the early weeks of the war was the Zouave uniform, whose resplendent colors enticed many young men to enlist.

In many states of the North in 1861, scores of companies and even regiments, calling themselves Zouaves, were seen wearing their peculiar uniform, a copy of the French Zouaves. The American outfit varied with different units, but generally included baggy Turkish trousers, a fez or turban, and bright colors throughout—with red dominating.

But hard-headed observers, both American and foreign, viewed the Zouave regalia with amused contempt. For example, a regiment of New York Zouaves landed on Ship Island and soon came under the unenthusiastic scrutiny of a taciturn Vermonter, General J. W. Phelps. It was not long before the General encountered one of the New Yorkers in his fantastic uniform. Phelps surveyed him with apparent surprise and asked curtly:

"Who are you?"

Federal Zouaves. 114th Pennsylvania Infantry guard mount at Brandy Station, Va., March 1864. (Courtesy Library of Congress)

"I'm a Zouave."

"What is that?"

"An officer of a Zouave regiment, sir."

"An officer! I thought you were a circus clown."

A British war correspondent, William Howard Russell, noted the "ridiculous" appearance of Duryea's Zouaves. In riding down the rear of this regiment in line, he was greatly amused at the "discolored napkins" tied around their heads, with no fez underneath, so that the hair stuck up through the folds. He found equally unmilitary the ill-made jackets, the "loose bags of red calico" hanging from the men's loins, and the long gaiters of white cotton—contrasting sharply with those worn by "real" Zouaves.

The net effect was that of a line of "military scarecrows," and Howard could hardly refrain from laughing outright.

More than fifty Zouave units have been identified as serving in the Federal Army. They were from the following states:

New York   17
Pennsylvania   11

Zouave group in camp. U.S. Signal Corps
photo, Brady Collection. (Courtesy The
National Archives)

Group of Ellsworth's Zouaves. U.S. Signal
Corps photo, Brady Collection. (Courtesy
The National Archives)

Wisconsin	8
Ohio	7
Massachusetts	3
Illinois	2
Indiana	2

And one each came from the following states: Kentucky, Missouri, Michigan, Kansas, New Jersey, Maine, Rhode Island, and the District of Columbia.

Many of these units were Zouaves in name only; they did not wear a Zouave uniform, or left no record of their uniforms. As for those regiments which did wear a Zouave outfit, almost all soon discarded the distinctive uniform for the regulation blue. This change was due to the fact that the Zouave uniform was too distinctive on the battle line and, moreover, soon wore out in a few months anyway.

With a few exceptions, the Zouave regiments were ineffective in combat. Not only were they at a disadvantage because of their conspicuous uniforms, but also many Zouave regiments attracted the less stable elements in some communities. For example, after the Battle of Williamsburg, a strapping big fellow with turbaned head, blue jacket profusely decorated with gold lace, and baggy red trousers, entered the camp of the 57th Pennsylvania Infantry.

"Hello! What regiment?" asked one of the 57th.
"——regiment."
"But what state?"
"New York, of course."
"In the fight?"
"Yep. All cut to pieces. I'm the only one left."

NEW YORK

Duryea's Zouaves (5th New York Infantry)
Despite the critical comments of William Howard Russell, this developed into a magnificent-looking regiment, with a color guard, some of whom were nearly seven-footers in height, all wearing the scarlet fez and uniform of the French Zouaves.

"Wilson's Zouaves" (6th New York Infantry)
This regiment (notoriously inefficient, by the way!) wore gray jackets furnished by the state. Details on the rest of the uniform are not available, except that it was made of extremely shoddy material.

"Hawkins' Zouaves" (9th New York Infantry)
Wore an easy-fitting uniform, permitting full action of body and arms. The trousers and jacket were "army blue," the trousers slightly full, plaited at the waist, with a magenta braid down the outer seam; jacket and vest had magenta trimmings, a sash of the same color of woolen material, wide enough to cover the stomach of the wearer; white leggings, and red fez with a blue tassel.

"National Zouaves" (10th New York Infantry)
Originally this regiment wore a dark brown Zouave uniform with red trimmings. In October 1861, it received a new Zouave uniform, consisting of light blue trousers, dark brown jacket, red vest, fez, and white canvas leggings. The jacket and trousers were trimmed with red. This uniform fitted easily but yet not too loosely.

"Ellsworth's First Fire Zouaves" (11th New York Infantry)
The most celebrated of all Zouave units was the 11th New York Infantry under the command of the youthful Colonel Elmer Ellsworth. This crack outfit, famous for its precision drill and iron discipline, originally wore a red fatigue cap, open blue jacket with yellow trimmings, loose red trousers tucked midway of the calf into leather leggings, and high shoes. It soon discarded most of the original uniforms and adopted a uniform of red shirt, gray jacket, red trousers, red cap, and tan calfskin gaiters.

Officer's Zouave uniform. Col. Rush Hawkins, 9th New York Infantry (Hawkins' Zouaves). U.S. Signal Corps photo, Brady Collection. (Courtesy The National Archives)

"Brooklyn Regiment" (14th New York Infantry)

This regiment wore a blue coat, blue cap trimmed with red, red trousers, and white gaiters.

"Ellsworth's Avengers" (44th New York Infantry)

Only the privates of this regiment wore the Zouave outfit; all officers—both commissioned and noncommissioned—wore the regulation uniform. The Zouave uniform as worn by the privates in this regiment consisted of a blue cap, Zouave jacket with brass buttons, blue trousers with red stripes on the outer seams, yellow leggings, and linen havelocks. The Zouave outfit was worn only a short time; soon, all members were wearing the regulation uniform.

"Anderson's Zouaves" (62nd New York Infantry)

In October 1861, this regiment, nicknamed the "Advanced Zoos," had such a bad reputation that the "Zou-Zous" brought discredit on all wearers of the Zouave uniform. The 62nd New York was known for its sloppiness and thievery. The men robbed friend and foe alike and antagonized the general public as well as other regiments. The camps of this Zouave regiment were constantly covered with filth and rubbish.

"Halleck Infantry" (146th New York Infantry)

In contrast to the 62nd was the 146th New York Infantry, an excellent regiment whose Zouave uniforms resembled closely that worn by the 5th and 140th New York Infantry regiments. On June 3, 1863, the 146th received its new uniform and the men were greatly

Zouave bandsmen. (Courtesy Library of Congress)

pleased by its comfort and utility—much superior to the regulation uniform they had been wearing. The new outfit consisted of large baggy blue trousers, a bright red fez with red tassel, white cloth leggings extending almost to the knees, and a red sash—ten feet long—which provided comfort and warmth. Also issued was a long white turban, used only on dress parade, when it was wrapped around the fez cap. Men experienced great difficulty learning to wrap the turban correctly but finally, "after much perspiring and considerable profanity, the entire regiment looked not unlike the soldiers of Mahomet."

"Duryee's Zouaves" (165th New York Infantry)

This regiment, formed from the former "Duryea Zouaves," retained the Zouave officer uniforms only. They consisted of the braided Zouave jacket, with cap, vest, and scarlet trousers.

PENNSYLVANIA

"Birney Zouaves" (23rd Pennsylvania Infantry)

Wore a dark blue Zouave uniform, greatly liked by the men. However, after six months' use, this uniform began to wear out and was replaced with a dark blue uniform, brass shoulder scales, and "dog collar." As a member bitterly expressed the men's reaction: "My, what a contrast from the natty Zouave suit to this one of misfits."

"Baxter's Philadelphia Fire Zouaves" (72nd Pennsylvania Infantry)

The uniform was picturesque but "not nearly as showy and foreign as that of the New York Zouaves." It consisted of light-blue pants with red cord at the side, a cutaway jacket, with rows of bright bell buttons, a hook and eye at the throat, a shirt of blue color (often with the company letter embroidered on the chest), regulation cap, and white leggings. But the men did not like the white leggings because they were too conspicuous on the skirmish line and at night. By the Peninsular Campaign most of the men had discarded their bright outfits in favor of the regulation uniform. At Gettysburg the 72nd was completely attired in the regulation uniforms. The statue of the 72nd soldier at Gettysburg (showing the soldier in a Zouave uniform) merely symbolizes the regiment's original Zouave organization and uniform.

"Collis' Zouaves" (114th Pennsylvania Infantry)

As a special mark of merit, this regiment was permitted to wear its Zouave uniform throughout its entire term of service in the Army of the Potomac. The uniform adopted consisted of red trousers, Zouave jacket, white leggings, blue sash around the waist, and a white turban. The net result for the regiment was unique and imposing. Material for the uniforms was imported from France and special arrangements were made to secure a sufficient supply of this material to replenish the uniforms during the whole term of service.

155th Pennsylvania Infantry

Men of this regiment were proud of their uniform but soon learned a major drawback. When they straggled, they were quickly identified as members of the 155th because of their distinctive uniform. This consisted of wide, dark blue knee breeches; heavy, dark blue jacket, trimmed with yellow at the collar, wrists, and down the front; red flannel sash, ten feet long and about ten inches wide, trimmed with yellow, wound around the waist; white canvas leggings, reaching halfway to the knees; turban "of the Turkish model," composed of a white flannel sash about a foot wide and ten feet long, to be worn on dress occasions, and replaced by a

Cartridge box plate of 114th Pennsylvania
Infantry "Zouaves d'Afrique." (Courtesy
Francis A. Lord)

Havelock. (Courtesy Mike McAfee)

Officer's overcoat. Captain Thomas D. Connor, Company "D" 45th Illinois Infantry, killed at Shiloh, April 6, 1862. (Courtesy Jack Meyer, Urbana, Illinois)

red fez cap with tassel on all other occasions.

This unusual Zouave outfit was exceedingly popular with the home folks. The fancy drills of the 155th as well as its presence at flag presentations and reviews were always attended by large crowds of civilians. The regiment was especially popular with teenage schoolboys.

The 155th along with the 140th New York, 146th New York, and 91st Pennsylvania Infantry regiments, comprised the 3rd Brigade, 2nd Division, 5th Army Corps. This brigade was a Zouave brigade—the only one in the Federal army—and all regiments wore the Zouave uniform in the latter part of the war.

MASSACHUSETTS

"Salem Zouaves" (8th Massachusetts Infantry)

This militia unit wore a modified Zouave uniform, consisting of dark blue jacket and trousers, trimmed with scarlet braid, white leggings, and red fatigue caps.

23rd Massachusetts Infantry

The uniform adopted consisted of Zouave jacket of gray flannel faced with blue, dark blue trousers and gray cap, all trimmed with red. The officers wore a single-breasted frock coat (collar and cuffs of blue), and dark blue trousers; blue straight visored cap which, like the coat, was trimmed with gold braid.

Eventually the men had to give up their Zouave uniforms because of the theft of turkeys by some Company "A" men. The colonel made the decision to turn in the uniforms because he did not want his men to be caught again! The Zouave uniforms had pinned the blame on his unit, whereas a less conspicuous uniform would not have been so easily traced.

INDIANA

Zouave regiments were not popular in several Western states. The conspicuous nature of gaudy uniforms apparently did not appeal to men, who, closer to frontier life, realized the foolishness of giving the enemy such good targets to shoot at. The most famous Zouave unit from the West was that led by Lew Wallace, known to posterity as the author of *Ben Hur*.

"Wallace Zouaves" (11th Indiana Infantry)
Formed in 1861, this Zouave regiment

avoided the flashy uniforms of Eastern Zouave units. Instead, the 11th Indiana was uniformed in the "tamest gray twilled goods not unlike home-made jeans"; a French-type visor cap with a top of red cloth about the size of the palm of the hand; a blue flannel shirt with open neck; a jacket "Greekish in form,"

Soldier of the 4th New Hampshire Infantry. (Courtesy Mike McAfee)

edged with narrow binding and the red scarcely noticeable; breeches "baggy but not petticoated"; button gaiters connecting below the knees with the breeches, and strapped over the shoe. The net effect was to magnify the men. Even when in line, at a distance of 2,000 yards the men looked like "a smoky ribbon long drawn out."

CHASSEURS

Like the Zouaves, the origin of these troops

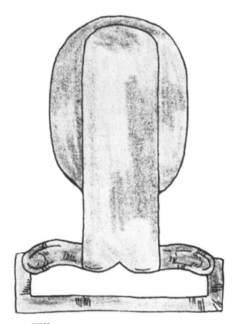

Militia belt buckle, dug up at Hilton Head Sept. 4, 1966. (Courtesy Carol Ruckdeschel)

are to be found in special French units. The term "chasseurs" means "hunters" and was applied to various forms of light troops in the French service, organized at different times, either as infantry or cavalry. Similar to the "Jaegers" of Austria and certain Italian units, the "chasseurs" were copied by a few Federal regiments. Of the six such units identified, five were from New York, one from Pennsylvania.

12th New York Infantry

On May 8, 1861, the regiment received the Chasseur uniform which observers found to present a very soldierly appearance. This uniform consisted of long, dark-blue coats, light blue baggy trousers, and a modified fatigue cap.

1st U. S. Chasseurs (65th New York Infantry)

Available information on the outfit of this regiment merely states that the men wore a "natty uniform." However, as with the 12th New York and other chasseur units, details are lacking. But, like the Zouaves, these men in regiments of chasseurs soon gave up their distinctive outfits and donned the regulation uniform.

The Erie Regiment (83rd Pennsylvania Infantry)

This fighting regiment, which McClellan complimented as being "one of the very best regiments in the army," was awarded the honor of wearing the "Chasseur de Vincennes" uniform imported from France. Each soldier received a shako, two jaunty suits—dress and fatigue—cloak, two pairs of shoes, two pairs of white gloves, two nightcaps, gaiters, and a small bag containing five brushes for various purposes, needle case, combs, thread, spool, cloak pin, and various other

Corporal Jacob T. Shriner, Co. "G" 83rd Pennsylvania Infantry. This photo shows Shriner in the uniform of a "chasseur de Vincennes"—a uniform imported from France. Shriner was mortally wounded at Hanover Court House, Va., and died June 10, 1862. (Courtesy H. W. Strawbridge, Diamond, Pa.)

items. No details as to color of the uniform are available. Since these uniforms were made originally for Frenchmen, it was soon observed that the uniforms were not large enough for most of the Pennsylvanians who, on the whole, were larger than the French. When the 83rd left for the Peninsula in the spring of 1862, these French uniforms were packed up and stored in a warehouse in Georgetown, D.C.

3

Special U.S. Units

SPECIAL CAVALRY UNITS

"Rush's Lancers" (6th Pennsylvania Cavalry)
This unique unit wore the regulation cavalry uniform.

"1st U.S. Hussars" (3rd New Jersey Cavalry)
Although they liked the title of "Hussars," the regiment was better known as the "Butterflies." The regiment was called "Butterflies" because of the gaudy effect of their uniforms; especially the hussar jackets which were overloaded with yellow braid. The nickname "Butterflies" had more than a tinge of contempt. In the critical cavalry fight at Yellow Tavern the "Butterflies" retreated in mad haste when they came under Confederate artillery fire. Later, a major of this unit rallied some of his "Butterflies," explaining that the shells had stampeded their horses and the men had gone looking for them. But an observer, T. W. Hyde of the 7th Maine Infantry, was unimpressed. "We had many kinds of material in the Army of the Potomac and use for most of it, but not for the 'Uhlanen'."

COLORED TROOPS

"Corps d'Afrique" (United States Colored Troops)
According to the Army Appropriation Bill of June 15, 1864, "all persons of color . . . [in] the military service of the United States shall receive the same uniform, clothing, arms, equipments . . . as other soldiers of the regular or volunteer forces of the United States of [the same branch of service]."

The only exception was in the matter of shoes. For example, on April 9, 1863, the Secretary of War was asked to have 10,000 pairs of "Negro shoes of large size" sent to Memphis, Tennessee. There are various references to "Negro brogans" in the reports of requisitioning officers during the war period. Apparently these were similar to the shoes worn by field hands on the plantations and were generally roomy and simple in construction.

However, the uniforming of colored troops aroused resentment among the white troops. When the Government decided to arm the Negroes, it was with great difficulty that the Quartermaster Department met the requisitions for organizing a hundred regiments. It was necessary to depart from the accustomed uniform material for volunteers. Instead of the coarse material issued to new white regiments, colored troops received uniforms of excellent quality. The new uniforms of the colored troops put the threadbare clothes of the white veterans in sad contrast and was the cause of many a black soldier being badly treated by white soldiers. As for example,

Battery squad on drill. U.S. Signal Corps photo, Brady Collection. (Courtesy The National Archives)

Joseph T. Wilson, a member of the 54th Massachusetts Infantry (colored) had half his clothes torn off in New Orleans by two white soldiers of the 24th Connecticut Infantry.

Some Negroes enlisted readily because they could choose the arm of service for the color which appealed most to them; some preferring one color, some another—choosing the infantry for its blue, the artillery for its red, the cavalry for its yellow. "When a young Negro has enlisted, and returns in full regimentals to bid his friends goodbye, he struts like a turkey cock . . . while the old men and women throw up their hands with a hundred benedictions, the girls languish for a glance of his eye, and the children run after him in wonder with their mouths and eyes wide open."

INVALID CORPS
(Name changed to "Veteran Reserve Corps" March 18, 1864)

One of the first steps of the War Department with regard to this unique organization was to devise a special uniform for it. For enlisted men it consisted of a dark-blue forage cap and sky-blue trousers, according to the regulation infantry uniform. The men wore a sky-blue jersey jacket, trimmed with dark blue and cut long in the waist, like that of the U.S. Cavalry. Officers wore a sky-blue frockcoat, with collar, cuffs, and shoulder strap background of dark blue velvet, and sky-blue trousers, with a double stripe of dark blue down the outer seam, the stripes half an inch wide and three-eights of an inch apart.

Although the uniform was attractive, it never became popular with the wearers. The men resented being distinguished from line units by this special uniform; they wanted to keep the dark-blue blouse and dress coat in which they had learned their profession and received their honorable disability. This feeling was sharply aggravated by the inevitable jealousy between front-line troops and rear-echelon soldiers. Eventually this jealousy developed into a definite bitterness between the Invalid Corps soldiers and the men of the units in which the Invalid Corps men had originally marched and fought.

In the case of the officers, the light blue was unattractive to the eye, and soiled so easily that eventually the officers were directed to resume the wearing of the dark-blue frockcoat, although retaining the other insignia of their branch of the service.

ENGINEERS

Although there were several engineer units, both regular and volunteer, in the Federal Army, the "castle" was worn only by Company "A" Engineer Battalion of the Regular Army. This insignia—worn only by the very few men comprising Company "A"—passed the men anywhere around Washington. However, later the addition of two volunteer units, the 15th and 50th New York Engineers, as well as new regular engineer companies, increased the number to more than 2,000. But the privilege was sometimes imposed on. Accordingly, Captain Duane in January 1862, took the castles from the caps of the battalion

men as the best solution to the difficulty.

On May 24, 1863, castles and letters were again issued to the battalion.

ARMY AMPHIBIOUS UNITS

Ellet's Mississippi Marine Brigade

This unique organization consisted of one infantry regiment (10 companies), one cavalry battalion (4 companies), and a 6-gun light artillery battery. Its personnel were recruited from convalescents from army hospitals. The men were promised no long marches, no trenches to dig, no picket duty, and no chance of short rations! They operated from river gunboats and kept the banks clear of enemy guerrillas attempting to fire on Federal boats.

The uniform was the same as that worn in the army, except for the caps, which were made with full, round tops, broad straight visors, and a wide green band with trimmings of gold lace.

1st New York Marine Artillery

The uniform of this regiment was very similar to that of the navy. The officers wore a gold band on the cap, but no sash under the sword belt. The shoulder strap was red, with a crossed cannon and anchor wrought in silver. (This emblem was later adopted by General A. E. Burnside's 9th Army Corps). Line officers wore double-breasted coats. Enlisted men wore a dark navy blue uniform. Arms were short Belgian rifles and sword bayonets for men who served as infantry, while pistols and cutlasses were issued to the men who worked the howitzers.

SHARPSHOOTERS

1st United States Sharpshooters

This unique regiment wore a distinctive uniform, consisting of coat, blouse, pants, and cap of green cloth. Leather leggings, buckling as high as the knee, were worn by officers and men alike. The men also carried the Prussian knapsack—leather tanned with the hair on, and a small cooking kit strapped on the outside.

"Thus equipped the regiment was distinctive in its service, and soon became well known in the army."

Officers wore green shoulder straps and a green regulation-type cap with "U.S.S.S." in gold surrounded by a gold wreath.

A very young Federal soldier, Sergeant John L. Clem, aged twelve, of Michigan. This uniform was obviously specially made. (Courtesy Southern Historical Collection)

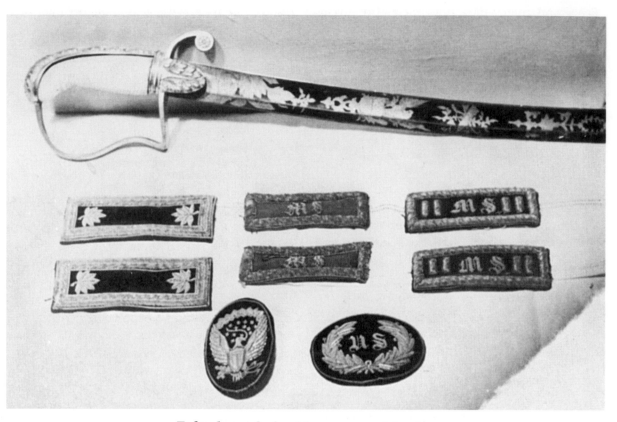

Federal sword, shoulder straps, and hat insignia worn by Surgeon Edward S. Walker, 34th New York Infantry. (Courtesy Mrs. D. C. Markham, Worthington, Mass.)

BRIGADE UNIFORMS

"Irish Brigade" (1st Div., 2nd Corps)

This famous unit wore gray trousers, and blue jackets with green collars and green shoulder straps.

The regiments of this brigade were: 63rd, 69th, 88th New York, 28th Massachusetts, and 116th Pennsylvania regiments of infantry.

"Iron Brigade" (1st Div., 1st Army Corps)

In the fall of 1861, this brigade drew the full uniform of the regular army. The 2nd Wisconsin Infantry was the first to get the Jefferson Davis hat (also called the Kossuth hat), looped up on one side and "garnished with cord and brasses and feather"—the headgear of the regulars in 1861. This regiment was thereby dubbed the "Black Hats." The other regiments in the brigade followed suit.

With its unique headgear (in sharp contrast to the other Eastern units which wore the kepi), members of this brigade were recognized at once by friend and foe alike. At Gettysburg, the Confederates advanced against the Iron Brigade, thinking they were confronted only by militia. When Archer's Confederate brigade met the Iron Brigade, some of the Confederates were heard to exclaim: "There are those d----d black-hatted fellows again; 'taint no militia, it's the Army of the Potomac." No other regiments in the Army of the Potomac wore the Jeff Davis hat. This brigade—one of the best in the Army of the Potomac—was composed of the 2nd, 6th, 7th Wisconsin, 19th Indiana, and 24th Michigan Infantry.

BALLOON CORPS

The military aeronauts enjoyed a quasi-military status. Although they served at the front and frequently came under enemy fire, they were rated as civilian employees and had no command functions of a military nature. Families of aeronauts received no pensions in case of the death of an aeronaut, and the aeronauts were technically liable to execution as spies if captured. Aeronauts wore ordinary civilian clothes that were suitable for field service. A few aeronauts wore "B.C." (Balloon Corps) or "A.D." (Aeronautic Department) as insignia on their headgear. These insignia were never official and the aeronauts soon discarded them as they only provoked amusement.

TELEGRAPH CORPS

Normally, military telegraphers did not wear uniforms; they were civilians. However, several complained that because they served with the military forces they were entitled to wear a uniform. They pointed out that they were constantly being treated as mere civilians by junior officers who, motivated by jealousy, often subjected them to unnecessary and petty annoyances. To overcome this treatment and to improve the telegraphers' morale, General George H. Thomas, commanding the Department of the Cumberland, issued (March 26, 1864) General Order No. 51 which provided that:

The Telegraph Operators within this De-partment are hereby authorized to wear an undress uniform as follows:

Blouse—dark blue

Trousers—dark blue cloth, with silver cord, one-eighth of an inch in diameter, along the outer seam.

Vest—buff, white or blue.

Forage Cap—like that worn by commissioned officers, but without any distinctive mark or ornament.

Buttons—like those worn by officers of the General Staff.

This order resulted in the operators being treated as officers by all personnel not personally acquainted with them. However, it was amusing to note the embarrassment of officers and soldiers in their vain attempts to recognize operators by their proper rank. Often the operators were given much higher rank than even they expected. Since telegraph operators served directly with the generals at headquarters as staff personnel, it was not uncommon for the telegraph operators to be treated as colonels. Eventually the post operators reverted to wearing no uniforms to avoid the incessant query as to their actual rank. Many operators in the field, however, wore a uniform right up to the war's end.

On July 5, 1864, General McPherson, commanding the Department of the Tennessee, issued an order similar to that for the Department of the Cumberland, except that it authorized the wearing of a small silver cord around the cap band.

PROVOST-MARSHALS

The uniform of the provost-marshals, when engaged in the duties of their office, shall be that of a captain of the general staff, as prescribed in Army Regulations.

CHAPLAINS

By Congressional act of July 17, 1862, the rank of chaplain, without command, in the

Chaplain Thomas Scully. (Courtesy Library of Congress)

Chaplain Gordon Winslow, 5th New York
Infantry. (Courtesy Library of Congress)

Chaplains of the 9th Army Corps, October
1864. (Courtesy Library of Congress)

United States service, was recognized. Chaplains were to be borne on the field and staff rolls next after the surgeons, and should wear such uniform as was or would in the future be prescribed by Army Regulations. They were to be subject to the same rules and regulations as other officers of the army.

Uniform for chaplains was prescribed by General Order No. 102 (November 25, 1861). It called for a plain black frockcoat with standing collar, and one row of nine black buttons; plain black trousers; black felt hat or army forage cap, without ornament. On occasions of ceremony, a plain chapeau de bras could be worn. On August 25, 1864, the

uniform regulations for chaplains was amended by General Order No. 247 as follows: The coat was to have "herring bone" of black braid around the buttons and button holes; a hat or cap insignia was to be worn, consisting of a gold embroidered wreath, on black velvet ground, encircling the letters U.S. in silver, old English characters.

But, despite these specific regulations, there remained confusion all through the war as to the rank, uniform, and duties of chaplains. Many chaplains adopted the ordinary uniform of a captain of cavalry, with shoulder straps, sash, and sword.

Some chaplains never did learn their uni-

Chaplain Joseph F. Sutton, 102nd New
York Infantry. (Courtesy Library of Congress)

form regulations. As late as 1893, Chaplain Frederic Denison, 1st Rhode Island Cavalry wrote:

It was certainly a mistake that the uniform and arms of chaplains were not laid down by military regulations. So far as outward appearance was concerned, it was sometimes difficult to distinguish chaplains from sutlers or civilians. No reason exists why a chaplain in war time should not be distinguishable by his dress, like any other officer; nor why he should not be prepared to act upon the defensive. Surgeons, quar-

termasters, adjutants, and all aid[e]s wear arms. Why should not chaplains? If they exhort men to fight, why not fight themselves, if they have a chance? [Later he was presented with a sword and sword belt—wore them in combat and captured six Confederates while so armed.]

Chaplain Horatio S. Howell, 90th Pennsylvania Infantry, was killed in front of the Lutheran Church in Gettysburg during the retreat of the Federals, July 1, 1863. He refused to surrender to a Confederate infantryman, who shot Howell because the chaplain

Chaplain Thomas H. Mooney, 69th New York Infantry, Arlington, Va. (Courtesy Library of Congress)

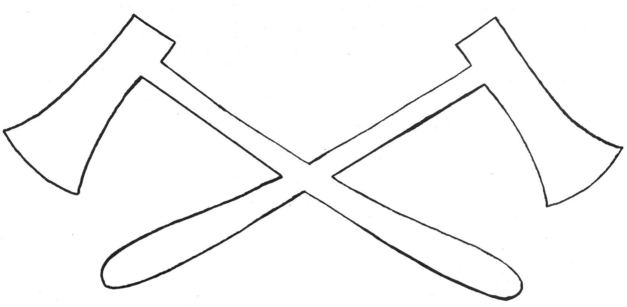
Pioneer Corps insignia. (Courtesy Mike McAfee)

was wearing a sword and appeared to be a line officer and not a noncombatant.

The confusion occasioned by chaplains' uniforms provided considerable amusement to the troops. At times chaplains were utilized to perform functions not entirely compatible with their religious duties. For example, on one occasion the chaplain of the 34th Massachusetts Infantry wanted to get some whiskey to break up a bad cold. But since only commissioned officers wearing shoulder straps could purchase whiskey, the chaplain asked the colonel to issue an order permitting him to wear shoulder straps. When asked why he —a chaplain—should wear shoulder straps, the chaplain pointed out that he drew pay equal to that of a captain of cavalry. And, the chaplain continued, the surgeon had already prescribed whiskey for his cold. The chaplain got his order and his whiskey.

Sometimes other officers used the chaplain's uniform to provide humor. A surgeon, who always wore a coat with black buttons, was nicknamed the chaplain by his men. He liked the good things of life and only his non-regulation coat bore any relationship to the office of a chaplain. One day, in winter quarters, the chaplain of a Massachusetts regiment called at the tent of the surgeon's commanding officer and inquired for the chaplain. The colonel, who liked a practical joke, directed the chaplain to the surgeon's tent. The chaplain entered the tent and extended his hand to the officer, who wore the black buttons and addressed him as chaplain.

The surgeon saw the joke and chatted fraternally with the chaplain for an hour. Everything went smoothly until the chaplain inquired of the surgeon as to the spiritual condition of the regiment. The surgeon replied that the spiritual condition was very bad despite all his labors of love for the men. "The infernal devils are bound to go to ruin anyway." The chaplain, with a look of horror at such language, left the camp in great haste.

MEDICAL CADETS

The uniform for medical cadets was as follows:

Coat—same as for brevet second lieutenant.

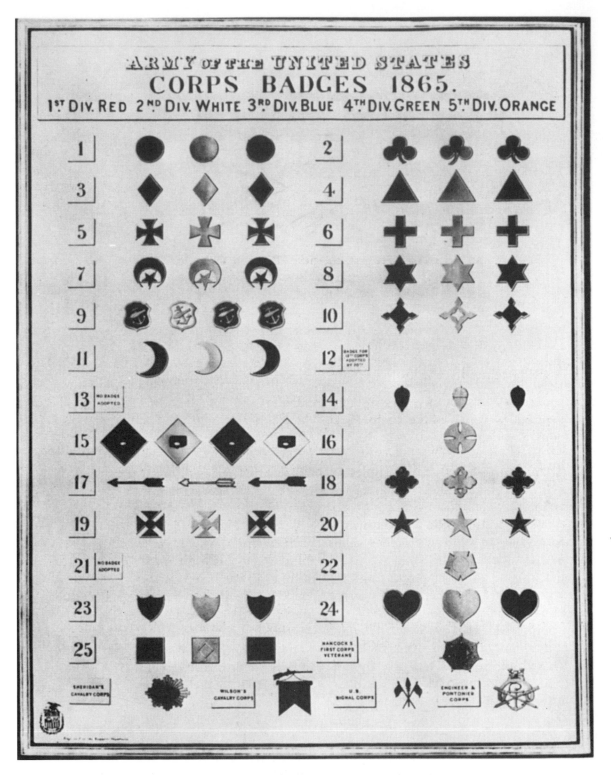

Federal Corps badges. (Courtesy The National Archives)

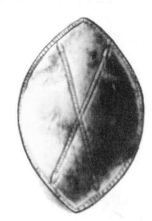

Rare Federal insignia: Birney's Brigade,
Rush's Lancers, Corcoran's Legion. (Courtesy Francis A. Lord)

Buttons—same as for the General Staff.

Trousers—same as for officers of the General Staff, except a welt of buff cloth was
substituted for the gold cord.

Headgear—forage cap or hat. Trimmings
for the hat were the same as for field
officers.

Sash—medium or emerald green silk net
with silk bullion fringe ends.

Sword—sword, belt, and belt plate were the
same as for noncommissioned officers.

Shoulder straps—a strip of gold lace 3
inches long, ½ inch wide, placed in the
middle of a strap of green cloth 3¾
inches by 1¼ inches wide.

NURSES' UNIFORM

Male nurses were drawn mainly from older
enlisted men of the army. As such, they wore
the regulation army uniform.

Female nurses normally wore their civilian
garb in their hospital assignments. Dorothea
Dix, superintendent of United States hospital
nurses, would accept only plain-looking wom-
en. They had to wear black or brown dresses
with no hoops. Fancy adornment, such as
jewelry or curls, was forbidden.

Some nurses enjoyed a semi-military status.
Adelaide W. Smith, an independent volunteer nurse, wore a dress of officers' blue, with
infantry buttons, medical cadet shoulder
straps with green bands and gilt braid in the
center. Another nurse, a Mrs. Daily, was a
colonel on the staff of Governor Sprague of
Rhode Island. She made tours of inspection,
visiting sick soldiers in different hospitals.

4

U.S. Navy, Marine Corps, Revenue-Cutter Service

NAVY

Information on Navy (and Marine Corps) uniforms has been gleaned from regulations of the 1850's and 1860's, and from catalogues of commercial uniform establishments. Among the latter are such firms as Schuyler, Hartley, and Graham; Horstmann; and Tomes, Melvain and Company.

The uniform of the Federal Navy during the Civil War was essentially as prescribed by the March 1852 uniform regulations. These regulations were later amended, and also altered by a new Uniform Regulation on January 28, 1864. By the 1852 order, sleeve lace was used to indicate officers' ranks, and various changes to the order directed that certain staff officers wear the same lace as the line officers with whom they held comparable rank. Actually, the trend was toward a common uniform and designating insignia for *all* officers of the Navy—line or staff—with identifications of corps being achieved by distinctive devices.

The January 28, 1864, regulations abolished "for the duration" epaulettes, cocked hats, and sword knots. The frockcoat with shoulder straps and the cap were prescribed as the uniform for all occasions. Rank and corps were shown on the shoulder straps.

With the expansion of the Navy during the Civil War, it soon became evident that a change was necessary in the rank structure itself. Accordingly, on July 16, 1862, the ranks of Rear Admiral, Commodore, Lieutenant Commander, and Ensign were established. To provide insignia for these new grades, the Government issued a general order on July 31, 1862, which modified the 1852 Uniform Regulations. By the new order, the use of the $\frac{3}{4}$-inch lace (as prescribed in 1852) was combined with the use of the $\frac{1}{4}$-inch lace. This arrangement was again modified on May 23, 1863. By this latest change, all lace was to be $\frac{1}{4}$-inch apart, unless $\frac{1}{2}$-inch spacing was prescribed. The star on the sleeve (prescribed earlier for "Lieutenants while on duty as Executive Officers"), became the designation of line officers.

All the changes effected in the Uniform Regulations after 1852 were embodied in the new Regulations issued on January 28, 1864. The only major change in the lace arrangement before the end of the Civil War was made especially for Rear Admiral D. G. Farragut. Upon his appointment as a Vice Admiral, Uniform Circular No. 1 of January 19, 1865, introduced the broad strip of 2-

inch lace presently worn by flag officers in the Navy. In lieu of the eight strips of 1/4-inch lace worn by a Rear Admiral, the Vice Admiral wore one stripe of 2-inch lace with two strips of 1-inch lace above the 2-inch lace. The Vice Admiral also wore three stars on his cap and collar, rather than the two stars of a Rear Admiral.

SERVICE DRESS APRIL 1861 TO JULY 31, 1862

Sea Officers

Flag Officers, i.e., Senior Captain of Navy and Commanders of Fleets or Squadrons

Coat—double-breasted frock coat, nine large buttons on each breast, rolling collar, full skirts. Three strips of 3/4 inch lace around sleeves.

Trousers—plain.

Shoulder straps—blue cloth, 4 inches long and 1 3/8 inches wide, gold embroidered border, 1/4 inch wide. Silver eagle and anchor in center, silver star at either end.

Cap—blue cloth, patent leather visor, gold lace band 1 1/2 inch wide. Cap device, silver eagle and anchor, in a wreath of oak and olive branches.

Captains

As Flag Officers, except for shoulder straps, the stars being omitted.

Commanders

Coat—as Captains, but with two strips of 3/4 inch lace on sleeves.

Trousers—plain.

Shoulder straps—as for Captain, but with two silver foul anchors crossed in center.

Cap—as Captain, but device in center of wreath to be two silver foul anchors, crossed.

Lieutenants

Coat—as Captain, but with one strip of lace on sleeves.

Trousers—plain.

Shoulder straps—as for Captain, but with single foul anchor in silver in center.

Cap—as Captain, but silver anchor in center of wreath.

Master

Coat—as Captain, but no lace on sleeves, three medium size buttons around top of cuffs.

Trousers—plain.

Shoulder straps—as Captain, but with no device.

Cap—as Captain, but with silver foul anchor in wreath, as Lieutenants.

Passed Midshipmen

Coat—as Captain, plain sleeves.

Trousers—plain.

Shoulder straps—gold lace, 4 inches long and 1/2 inch wide.

Cap—as Captain, but with silver foul anchor in wreath, as Lieutenant.

Midshipman

Coat—as Captain, but medium size instead of large buttons on breasts. Sleeves, plain.

Trousers—plain.

Shoulder straps—none.

Cap—as Captain, but a silver foul anchor in wreath, as Lieutenant.

Boatswain, Gunner, Carpenter and Sailmaker

Coat—double breasted frock coat, rolling collar, 8 large Navy buttons on each breast. On each side of collar, loop of gold lace to show 1 1/2 inch wide and 4 inches long, with a small button in point. Three medium sized buttons around top of cuff, with 2 small buttons in opening.

Trousers—plain.

Shoulder straps—none.

Cap—blue cloth, patent leather visor. Band 1 1/2 inch wide, 1/2 incn gold lace top and bottom, to show 1/2 inch dark blue between lace. Plain gold anchor.

Bill for a Uniform: Many Confederate Officers had their uniforms made by excellent tailors. This bill was rendered to Captain John C. Foster, 4th South Carolina Infantry. (Courtesy Lee's Studio, Lancaster, S.C.)

Masters Mates
Coat—blue cloth or flannel, rolling collar, single breasted, nine navy buttons on breast, none on cuffs.
Trousers—plain.
Shoulder straps—none.
Cap—blue cloth, patent leather visor, band 1½ inches wide, half inch wide gold lace top and bottom, showing ½ inch of blue cloth in center. Plain silver embroidered anchor above band, no wreath.

Shipped or Rated Masters Mates
Coat—blue cloth or flannel jacket, double-breasted, six medium-sized buttons on each breast, open fly sleeve, with three small buttons in the opening.
Trousers—plain.
Shoulder straps—none.
Cap—as other Masters Mates, without the band.

By 1864, the service uniform of the Federal Navy was as follows:

All officers wore a double-breasted frock-coat, with rolling collar and full skirts; nine large Navy buttons on each breast, unless otherwise noted. All shoulder straps, blue cloth, 4¼ inches long and 1½ inches wide, ¼ inch border of gold embroidery, unless noted.

LINE OFFICERS

Rear-Admiral

Sleeve ornaments—8 strips of ¼ inch gold lace, spaced ¼ inch apart, unless otherwise noted; ½ inch spacing between 1st and 2nd, 4th and 5th, 7th and 8th. Gold embroidered star above upper strip.

Shoulder strap devices—silver foul anchor in center, silver star each end.

Cap device—two silver stars in wreath of oak and olive branches.

Commodore

Sleeve ornaments—7 strips of ¼ inch gold lace, ¼ inch apart except, ½ inch between 3rd and 4th, and 4th and 5th. Gold star above upper strip.

Shoulder strap devices—silver star embroidered, a gold foul anchor, in center.

Cap device—silver foul anchor, set vertically, in wreath as Rear-Admiral.

Captain

Sleeve ornaments—6 strips of lace, with ½ inch space between 3rd and 4th. Gold star above top strip.

Shoulder strap devices—silver spread eagle, resting on anchor in center.

Cap device—as Commodore.

Commander

Sleeve ornaments—5 strips of lace, ½ inch space between 1st and 2nd, 4th and 5th. Gold star above top strip.

Shoulder strap devices—silver foul anchor in center, silver oak leaf each end.

Cap device—as Commodore.

Lieutenant Commander

Sleeve ornaments—4 strips of lace, ½ inch between 3rd and 4th. Gold star above top strip.

Shoulder strap devices—silver foul anchor in center, gold oak leaves each end.

Cap device—as Commodore.

Lieutenant

Sleeve ornaments—3 strips of lace, all ¼ inch apart.

Shoulder strap devices—silver foul anchor in center, with two gold bars at each end.

Cap device—as Commodore.

Master

Sleeve ornaments—two strips of lace, ¼ inch apart.

Shoulder strap devices—silver foul anchors in center, single gold bar at each end.

Cap device—as Commodore.

Ensign

Sleeve ornaments—single strip of ¼ inch lace, gold star above.

Shoulder strap ornaments—silver foul anchor in center, no end devices.

Cap device—as Commodore.

Gunner

Sleeve ornaments—gold embroidered star, approximately 3¼ inches above bottom of sleeve.

Shoulder strap devices—strap plain gold lace, 4 inches long and ¾ inch wide, no device.

Cap device—the wreath of oak and olive branches, without center device.

Boatswain

Sleeve ornaments—gold embroidered star, approximately 3¼ inches above bottom of sleeve.

Shoulder straps—plain gold lace 4 inches long, ¾ inch wide, with letter B, old English in silver, in center.

Cap device—wreath of oak and olive branches, no center device.

Carpenter
Sleeve devices—none.
Shoulder straps—plain gold lace 4 inches long, ¾ inch wide, with letter C, old English in silver in center.
Cap device—wreath of oak and olive branches, without center device.

Sailmaker
Sleeve ornaments—none
Shoulder straps—plain gold lace, 4 inches long, ¾ inch wide, no center device.
Cap device—wreath of oak and olive branches, without center device.

Midshipman (9 medium sized buttons on each breast)
Sleeve ornaments—gold embroidered star approximately 3¼ inches above bottom of sleeve.
Shoulder straps—none
Cap device—wreath of oak and olive branches, without center device.

Masters Mate (receiving $40.00 per month)
Coat—single breasted frock coat, rolling collar, nine medium sized buttons on the breast.
Sleeve ornaments—gold star approximately 3¼ inches above bottom of sleeve.
Shoulder Straps—none
Cap device—wreath of oak and olive, no center device.

Masters Mates, Yeoman, Master at Arms, Sergeants, Steward, Paymaster's Steward.
Coat—double breasted blue jacket, rolling collar, two rows of 6 medium buttons, slashed sleeves, four small buttons in openings.
Sleeve ornaments—none
Shoulder straps—none
Cap device—none

Cravat—for all officers, to be of black silk or satin, with a white shirt collar showing above it.

SWORD AND SCABBARD

For all officers, shall be a cut-and-thrust blade, not less than twenty-six nor more than twenty-nine inches long; half-basket hilt; grip white. Scabbards of black leather; mountings of yellow gilt.

SWORD-BELT

For all officers, shall be of plain black glazed leather, not less than 1½ inches nor more than two inches wide, with slings of the same not less than one half nor more than ¾ inch wide, and a hook in the forward ring to suspend the sword. Belt-plate of yellow gilt in front, two inches in diameter. The belt to be worn over the coat.

SWORD-KNOT

For a Captain and Commander, shall be blue and gold cord 24 inches long, including the tassel; gold and blue slide; tassel of 12 gold bullions 1¾ inches long, enclosing 5 blue bullions, with basket-worked head.

For all other Commissioned Officers, a strap of gold lace, one half inch wide and 18 inches long, including the tassel; gold slide; tassel of gold bullion, with basket-worked head.

N.B.-Sword-knots are dispensed with during the war.

BUTTONS

Shall be gilt, convex, and of three sizes in exterior diameter: large ⅞ inch; medium, 7/10 inch; and small, 9/16 inch. Each size is to have the same device.

Federal sailors off duty. (Courtesy Library of Congress)

SERVICE DRESS FOR PETTY OFFICERS AND CREW
(Approved January 28, 1864)

Boatswain's mates, gunner's mates, carpenter's mates, sailmaker's mates and ship's cook, will wear, embroidered in white silk, on the right sleeve of their blue jackets, above the elbow, in front, an eagle and anchor, of not more than three inches in length, with a star of one inch in diameter one inch above. The same device, embroidered in blue, to be worn on the sleeves of their white frocks in summer.

All other petty officers, except officers' stewards, will wear the same device on their left sleeves.

The outside clothing for petty officers, fire- *men, and coal-heavers, seamen, ordinary seamen, landsmen, and boys,* for muster, shall consist of blue cloth jackets and trousers, or blue woolen frocks; black hats; black silk neckerchiefs, and shoes, or boots in cold weather. In warm weather it shall consist of white frocks and trousers; black or white hats, as the commander may for the occasion direct, having proper regard for the comfort of the crew; black silk neckerchiefs, and shoes; the collars and cuffs to be lined with blue cotton cloth, and stitched round with thread. Thick blue cloth caps, without visors, may be worn by the crew at sea, except on holidays or at muster.

It is strictly enjoined upon commandants of stations and commanding officers of the

Navy to see that the foregoing regulations are complied with in every respect, and to require all deviations from them to be corrected.

Identification of the insignia for enlisted men of the Federal Navy is difficult to establish. According to the Uniform Regulations of March 8, 1852, there were prescribed sleeve markings for petty officers, and crew. Boatswain's Mates, Gunner's Mates, Carpenter's Mates, Sailmaker's Mates, and Ship's Cooks wore these sleeve markings, embroidered in white silk, on the right sleeve of their blue jackets. These were located above the elbow in front, consisted of an eagle and anchor, of not more than three inches in length, with a star of one inch in diameter, one inch above. The same device, embroidered in blue, was worn on the sleeves of their white frocks, in summer. With the exception of officers' stewards and yeoman, other petty officers were directed to wear the same device on the left sleeve. The uniform of other crew members was a plain blue with no distinguishing features during the Civil War other than a black silk neckerchief.

However, this writer believes that distinguishing sleeve insignia *were* worn, to some extent at least, by Federal enlisted personnel of the Navy. In *Regulations for the Uniform of the United States Navy,* published in 1866, there are plates depicting "sleeve ornaments" for petty officers, captains of forecastle, boatswains' mates, master at arms, signal quartermaster and quartermaster, captains of taps, carpenters' mates, gunners' mates and quarter gunners, and sailmakers' mates. Each of these "sleeve ornaments" has a distinctive device, appropriate for the wearer's particular assignment. It is probable that these insignia were authorized to be worn during the war and their use continued after cessation of hostilities.

Buttons:

According to Navy Department orders, dated January 28, 1864, buttons

shall be gilt, convex, and of three sizes in exterior diameter: large, seven-eights of an inch; medium, seven-tenths of an inch; and small, nine-sixteenths of an inch. Each size to have the same device.

This applied to officers. For the enlisted men there is evidence that plain bone buttons were used during the 1850's. During the Civil War a black, concave button of hard rubber was used. This button, is handsomely decorated with the letters "U.S.N.", stars, and an anchor. A specimen in the author's collection is marked on the back: "Novelty Rubber Co. Goodyear's Patent, 1851, New York."

MARINE CORPS

Information on Marine Corps insignia is derived from the Regulations for the Uniform and *Dress of the Marine Corps of the United States* (October, 1859). These regulations, prepared by the Quarter Master's Department of the Marine Corps, were published by Charles Desilver, a publisher in Philadelphia.

For dress the field officers wore a chapeau with a red feather plume. Company officers and enlisted men wore a stiff leather shako and pompom. The shako device bore a brass plate, measuring 9 11/16 inches by 12 11/32 inches (with borders—11 inches by 12⅞ inches). On this plate was sup: imposed the well-known bugle (the current army designation for infantry) with an M inside the bugle ring to indicate Marines.

For service ashore a blue frock coat was worn with white cross belts.

Officers wore epaulettes or shoulder knots with insignia corresponding to their army counterparts. They also wore sleeve insignia of rank.

Insignia for enlisted men were as follows:

For Sergeant Major, Quarter Master Sergeant, Drum Major and Chief Musicians

Two rows of large size Marine buttons on the breast, seven in each row, placed at equal distances; the distance between each row, 5½ inches at top and 3½ inches at bottom; standing collar to rise no higher than to permit the chin to turn freely over it; to hook in front at the bottom, and slope thence up and backward at an angle of 30 degrees on each side, making the total opening in front, an angle of 60 degrees; two loops of yellow worsted half inch lace on each side of the collar, with one small Marine button at the end of each loop; the bottom loop 4½ inches long; the upper loop not to extend further back than the bottom loop, and the front of both loops to slope up and backwards, with the front of the collar, at an angle of 30 degrees, collar to be edged all around with a scarlet edging, except those of the Drum Major, Chief Musicians, and Musicians, which will be edged all around with white; plain round cuff, 3 inches deep; slash on the sleeve to be 6 inches long, and 2¼ inches wide at the points, and one and nine-tenths of an inch at the narrowest part of the curve; three loops of yellow worsted half inch lace, and three small Marine Buttons, one in the center of each loop, on the slash of the sleeve, loops on the sleeve 2 inches long, and 1⅛ inches wide; the slashed flap on the sleeve to be edged with scarlet on the ends and indented edges, those of the Drum Major, Chief Musicians, and Musicians, to be edged with white; pockets with three-pointed edges in the folds of the skirt, one button at the hip, one at the center of the pocket opening, and one at the bottom, making six buttons on the back and skirt of the coat; the pocket side edges to have one point at the center of the edge, and to curve thence up and down to the top and bottom, corresponding with slash on the sleeve; the pocket side edges to be edged with scarlet on the ends and indented edges; those of the Drum Major, Chief Musicians, and Musicians, to be edged with white. Lining of the coat black. Skirts full.

For Sergeants—same as for Sergeant Major, except that there shall be but two loops, and two small Marine buttons on the slash of the sleeve, and that the slash shall be shortened to correspond with the reduction of the number of loops.

For Corporals—same as for Sergeants.

For Privates—same as for Corporals.

The uniform coat of all enlisted men, except the Drum Major, Chief Musicians, and Musicians, shall be a double-breasted frock coat of dark indigo blue cloth, with skirt extending ¾ of the distance from the top of the hip to the bend of the knee. Skirts full.

For Drum Major, Chief Musicians and Musicians—a scarlet cochineal dyed cloth double-breasted frock coat, with skirt extending ¾ of the distance from the top of the hip to the bend of the knee.

For Musicians—same as for Privates, except that the coat shall be of scarlet cochineal dyed cloth, and the collar, slashes on the sleeves, and the pocket side edges on the skirt, shall be edged with white. Skirts full.

Chevrons

Shall be worn on the uniform coat above the elbow, points up, of yellow silk lace ½ inch wide, as follows:

For a Sergeant Major—three bars and an arc on a scarlet ground.

For a Quarter Master Sergeant—three bars and a tie on a scarlet ground.

For a Drum Major—three bars and a tie, with a star in the center on a scarlet ground.

For Sergeants—chevrons of yellow worsted ½ inch lace, placed above the elbow, points up, as follows: For First Sergeants, three bars and a lozenge, edged with scarlet; other Sergeants, three bars edged with scarlet.

For a Corporal—same as for Sergeants, except that the chevrons shall consist of two bars each.

Incidentally, Marine Corps chevrons always pointed *up*—never down as with the army.

Buttons

Buttons are not described in the regulations but are merely referred to as "Marine buttons," differentiated according to size. Apparently, there were initially only two sizes—"large" and "small." But in 1864 such firms as Schuyler, Hartley, and Graham were selling three sizes—designated as "Marine Coat," "Marine Jacket," and "Marine Vest."

UNITED STATES REVENUE-CUTTER SERVICE

Deck Officers

Captain's Full Dress—blue cloth frock coat, with rolling collar, double-breasted, lined with black silk, nine buttons on each lapel, two on upper part of skirt, and two on lower part of skirt; two strips of half-inch gold lace around the upper part of each cuff; two plain gold apaulettes; blue cloth Navy cap, with one band of gold lace, with ornament of Treasury shield within wreath in gold; with Navy regulation sword; black silk cravat or stock; buff, blue or white vest (according to the season), single-breasted, with nine buttons in front; blue pantaloons, with stripe of gold lace on outer seam, or white pantaloons, according to season.

Captain's Undress—same as full dress, sub-

Federal Navy gun crew. U.S. Signal Corps photo, Brady Collection. (Courtesy The National Archives)

98

Federal sailors. (Courtesy Library of Congress)

stituting for the epaulettes a shoulder strap on each shoulder, of blue cloth, with raised gold edging; in the center, two crossed foul anchors; all of them to be worked in gold.

First Lieutenant's Full Dress—same as captain, with the exception of one strip of lace on the cuff, and cap with one foul anchor, over shield, with wreath, all in gold.

Undress—the same as captain, with the same exceptions; shoulder strap to be with one foul anchor over shield, and two bars at each end; cap the same as in full dress.

Second Lieutenant—dress and undress as first lieutenant, omitting one bar at each end of shoulder strap.

Third Lieutenant—dress and undress as second lieutenant, omitting bars on shoulder straps.

ENGINEERS

Chief Engineers' Dress and Undress—same as first lieutenant. Shoulder strap of blue cloth, with raised gold edging, with gold wheel, surmounted by anchor; cap with band, with wheel surmounted by star within wreath, all in gold.

First Assistant Engineers—same as chief engineer, substituting three buttons on cuff, in lieu of lace; shoulder strap same as chief engineer, omitting anchor; cap with gold band, with wheel inside of wreath, omitting star.

Second Assistant—same as first assistant, omitting wheel on strap and cap.

Petty Officer's Dress—blue cloth jacket, with nine revenue buttons on each lapel, three under each pocket flap, and three on each cuff; white or blue pantaloons (according to season).

Seamen, firemen, coal-passers, stewards, cooks, and boys—white frock (according to season); white or blue trousers; blue mustering cap or sennet hat.

5

C.S. Army, Navy, Marine Corps

Although as early as 1862, Confederate soldiers were wearing uniforms of all colors and varying qualities, a series of specific uniform regulations were promulgated early in 1861. On May 25, 1861, the New Orleans *Picayune* announced the following:

UNIFORM OF THE CONFEDERATE STATES ARMY

Army regulations have been issued for the uniform adopted by the War Department of the Confederate States, and are as follows:

Coat—cadet gray cloth, short tunic, double-breasted, two rows of buttons down the breast, two inches apart at the waist, and widening towards the shoulders.

Pants—sky-blue cloth, made full in the leg.

Branch of Service—different branches of the service will be distinguished by the color of their trimmings—blue for infantry; red for artillery; yellow for cavalry.

Buttons—plain gilt, convex in form, ¾-inch diameter. Artillery—buttons stamped with the letter *A*. Infantry and cavalry—buttons bear only the number of the regiment.

General and Staff Officers—dress will be dark blue cloth, trimmed with gold.

Medical Department—black cloth, gold and velvet trimming.

Insignia—all indications of rank will be marked on collars and sleeves. Badges of "distinguished rank"—on collar only.

Brigadier-General—3 large stars
Colonel—2 large stars
Lt. Colonel—1 large star
Major—1 small star and 1 horizontal bar
Captain—3 small stars
1st Lt.—2 small stars
2nd Lt.—1 small star

General and Staff Officers' Buttons
Buttons of bright gilt, convex, rounded at the edge—a raised eagle at the center, surrounded by 13 stars. Exterior diameter of large-size button—1 inch; of small size—½ inch.

Engineers' Button—Engineer officers button will be the same as general and staff officers' except that instead of the eagle and stars, there will be a raised *E* in German text.

Line Officers' Buttons—Artillery, infantry, cavalry, riflemen—the button will be a plain gilt convex, with a large raised letter in the center—*A* for artillery, *I* for infantry, etc. The exterior diameter of a large-size button—⅞ of an inch; small size—½ inch.

Cap—no cap has yet been adopted.

C. S. UNIFORM

On June 6, 1861, the C. S. War Department issued General Orders No. 9, prescribing the uniform for the C. S. Army as follows:

Tunic (coat)—All officers shall wear a tunic of gray cloth, known as cadet gray; the skirt to extend half way between the hip and the knee; double-breasted for all grades.

Brigadier General Two rows of buttons on the breast, eight in each row, placed in pairs; the distance between the rows four inches at top and three inches at bottom; stand-up collar, to rise no higher than to permit the chin to turn freely over it; to hook in front at the bottom, and slope thence up and backward, at an agle of 30 degrees, on each side; cuffs 2½ inches deep on the upper side, there to be buttoned with three small buttons, and sloped upward to a point at a distance of four inches from the end of the sleeve; pockets in the fold of the skirt, with one button at the hip and one at the end of each pocket, making four buttons on the back and skirt of the tunic, the hip buttons to range with the lowest breast buttons.

Colonel The same as for a brigadier general, except that there will be only seven buttons in each row on the breast, placed at equal distances.

Lieutenant Colonel, major, captain, and lieutenant The same as for a colonel.

Officers of the Corps of Engineers—same as for the general staff, except that, in place of the eagle and the stars, there will be a raised *E* in German text.

Officers of artillery, infantry, riflemen, and cavalry—gilt, convex, plain with large raised letter in the center— *A* for artillery, *I* for infantry, *R* for riflemen, *C* for cavalry; large size, ⅞ inch in exterior diameter; small size ½ inch.

Aides-de-camp—may wear the button of the general staff, or of their regiments or corps, at their option.

Enlisted men—artillery, yellow, convex, large raised letter *A* in the center, three-quarters of an inch in exterior diameter. All other enlisted men—same as for artillery except that the number of the regiment, in large figures, will be substituted for the letter *A*.

Trousers

Uniform trousers for both officers and enlisted men will be of cloth throughout the year; made loose, and to spread well over the foot; of light (or sky) blue color for regimental officers and enlisted men; and of dark-blue for all other officers; re-enforced for the cavalry.

General officers—two stripes of gold lace on the outer seam, one-eighth of an inch apart, and each ⅝ inch wide.

Officers of Adjutant General's Department, Quartermaster-General's Department, Commissary-General's Department, Corps of Engineers—one stripe of gold lace on the outer seam, 1¼ inches in width.

Medical Department—a black velvet stripe, 1¼ inches in width, with a gold cord on each edge of the stripe.

Regimental Officers—a stripe of cloth on the outer seam, one inch and a quarter in width; color according to the corps—for artillery, red; cavalry, yellow; infantry, dark blue.

Noncommissioned officers—for noncommissioned staff of regiments and for all sergeants, a stripe of cotton webbing or braid on the outer seam, one inch and a quarter in width; color according to arm of service.

All other enlisted men—plain.

Chapeau (cocked hat)

Chapeau or cocked hat will be worn by general officers and officers of the general staff and Corps of Engineers, of what is called the French pattern; the model to be

CONFEDERATE TYPES OF 1862.

Confederate type of uniform, Artillery, 1862. U.S. Signal Corps photo, Brady Collection. (Courtesy The National Archives)

Maryland Guard, C.S.A.—a sketch. U.S.
Signal Corps photo, Brady Collection.
(Courtesy The National Archives)

deposited in the office of the Quartermaster-General.

Forage cap for officers, a cap similar in
form to that known as the French kepi, according to pattern to be deposited in the
office of the Quartermaster-General.

Uniform cap, according to pattern to be
desposited in the office of the Quartermaster-General.

Pompom
Artillery—red

Infantry—light blue
Cavalry—yellow

Cravat (or Stock)
All officers—black.
When a cravat is worn, the tie not to be
visible at the opening of the collar.
Enlisted men—black leather, according to
pattern.

Boots
All officers—ankle or Jefferson.

Cavalry enlisted men—ankle and Jefferson, according to pattern.

Other enlisted men—Jefferson, according to pattern.

Spurs

All mounted officers—yellow metal or gilt.

Enlisted mounted men—yellow metal, according to pattern.

Gloves

General officers and officers of the general staff and staff corps—buff or white

Officers of artillery, infantry, and cavalry—white

Sash

General officers—buff silk net, with silk bullion fringe ends; sash to go twice around

Private Confederate type of uniform. U.S. Signal Corps photo, Brady Collection. (Courtesy The National Archives)

Trooper of the Virginia Cavalry on horse.
A sketch—1861. U.S. Signal Corps photo,
Brady Collection. (Courtesy The National
Archives)

the waist and to tie behind the left hip; pendent part not to extend more than eighteen inches below the tie.

Officers of the general staff and engineers, artillery, infantry—red silk net.

Cavalry officers—yellow silk net.

Medical officers—green silk net.

All of these sashes will have silk bullion fringe ends; to go around the waist and to tie as for general officers.

Sergeants—worsted, with worsted bullion fringe ends; red for artillery and infantry, and yellow for cavalry; to go twice around the waist and to tie as above specified.

Sword Belt

For all officers, a waist belt, not less than one inch and a half nor more than two inches wide; to be worn over the sash; the sword to be suspended from it by slings of the same material as the belt, with a hook attached to the belt upon which the sword may be hung.

General officers—Russian leather, with three stripes of gold embroidery; the slings embroidered on both sides.

All other officers—black leather, plain.

Noncommissioned officers—black leather, plain.

Sword-Belt Plate

For all officers and enlisted men—gilt, rectangular; two inches wide, with a raised bright rim, a silver wreath of laurel encircling the "arms of the Confederate States."

Sword and Scabbard

For all officers—according to pattern to be deposited in the Ordnance Bureau.

Sword Knot

For all officers—of plaited leather, with tassels.

Badges to Distinguish Rank

On the sleeve of the tunic rank will be distinguished by an ornament of gold braid, extending around the seam of the cuff and up the outside of the arm to the bend of the elbow; to be of one braid for lieutenants, two for captains, three for field officers, and four for general officers; the braid to be $\frac{1}{8}$ inch in width.

On the front part of the collar of the tunic the rank of officers will be distinguished as follows:

General Officers—a wreath with three stars inclosed, embroidered in gold. The edge of the wreath to be $\frac{3}{4}$ inch from the front edge of the collar; the stars to be arranged horizontally, the center one to be one inch and a quarter in exterior diameter, and the others $\frac{3}{4}$ inch.

Colonel—three stars embroidered in gold, arranged horizontally and dividing equally the vertical space of the collar. Each star to be $1\frac{1}{4}$ inches in exterior diameter; the front star to be $\frac{3}{4}$ inch from the edge of the collar.

Lieutenant-Colonel—two stars of the same material, size and arrangement as for a colonel.

Major—one star of same material and size as for a colonel; to be placed $\frac{3}{4}$ inch from edge of collar, and dividing equally the vertical space.

Captain—three horizontal bars embroidered in gold; each $\frac{1}{2}$ inch in width; the upper bar to be 3 inches in length; the front edge of the bars to incline to correspond with the angle of the collar, and to be $\frac{3}{4}$ inch from the edge; the line of the back edges to be vertical.

First Lieutenant—two horizontal bars of same material and size as for captains, and dividing equally the vertical space of collar.

Second Lieutenant—one horizontal bar of same material and size as for the center bar of captain, and dividing equally the vertical space of collar.

Enlisted Men

Uniform coat, double-breasted tunic of

The Last of Ewell's Corps, by Frederic Ray

The original oil painting by Frederic Ray, art director of *Civil War Times Illustrated*, depicts a group of Confederates surrendering at Saylor's Creek. It is based on a sketch by Alfred R. Waud, dated April 6, 1865.

108

From an original oil painting by Frederic Ray, art director of *Civil War Times Illustrated,* titled "Stuart's Troopers." Mr. Ray points out that the method of carrying the sword shown in his painting is based on a sketch by W. L. Sheppard, a Confederate veteran.

gray cloth, known as cadet gray, with the skirt extending half way between the hip and the knee; two rows of buttons on the breast, seven in each row; the distance between the rows four inches at top and three inches at bottom; stand-up collar, to rise no higher than to permit the chin to turn freely over it; to hook in front at the bottom, and slope backward at an angle of 30 degrees on each side; cuffs two inches and a half deep at the upper seam, to button with two small buttons, and to be slightly pointed on the upper part of the arm; pockets in the folds of the skirt. The collars and cuffs to be of the color prescribed for facings for the respective arms of service, and the edges of the tunic to be trimmed throughout with the same colored cloth. Narrow lining in the skirt of the tunic of gray material.

Facings

General officers, and officers of the Adjutant General's Department, Quartermaster-General's Department, Commissary-General's Department, and Engineers—buff.
Other officers—tunic will be edged throughout with the following colored facings:
Medical Department—black.
Artillery—red.
Cavalry—yellow.
Infantry—light blue.
For fatigue purposes, a light-gray blouse, double-breasted, with two rows of small buttons, seven in each row; small turnover collar may be issued to the troops.
On all occasions of duty, except fatigue and when out of quarters, the coat will be buttoned and hooked at the collar. Officers on bureau duty may wear the tunic open.

Buttons

General officers, and officers of the general staff—bright gilt, rounded at the edge, con-

vex, raised eagle in the center, with stars surrounding it; large size, one inch in exterior diameter; small size, ½ inch.

Overcoats for enlisted men

Mounted men—of cadet gray cloth; stand-up collar; double-breasted; cape to reach to the cuff of the coat when the arm is extended, and to button all the way up. (Number of buttons—18.)
Foot troops—of cadet gray cloth; stand-up collar; double-breasted; cape to reach to the elbows when the arm is extended and to button all the way up (18 buttons). For the present, to be a talma, with sleeves, of waterproof material; black.

Chevrons

Rank of noncommissioned officers will be designated by chevrons on both sleeves of the uniform tunic and the overcoat, above the elbow, of silk or worsted binding half an inch wide; color the same as the edging of the tunic; points down, as follows:
Sergeant-Major—three bars and an arc in silk.
Quartermaster-Sergeant—three bars and a tie in silk.
Ordnance Sergeant—three bars and a star in silk.
First (Orderly) Sergeant—three bars and a lozenge in worsted.
Sergeant—three bars in worsted.
Corporal—two bars in worsted.

Hair and Beard

The hair will be short; the beard will be worn at the pleasure of the individual; but, when worn, to be kept short and neatly trimmed.
Because these regulations failed to prescribe for a cap and headgear rank designation, the Confederate States War Department issued General Orders No. 4,

January 24, 1862, prescribing the following:

Forage Cap
  Pattern—of the form known as the French kepi; to be made of cloth.
General Officers, Officers of the general staff, and engineers—dark blue band, sides, and crown.
Artillery—dark-blue band; sides and crown red.
Infantry—dark-blue band; sides and crown light blue.
Cavalry—dark-blue band; sides and crown yellow.

Marks to distinguish rank
  Four gold braids for general officers, three for field officers, two for captains, and one for lieutenants, to extend from the band on the front, back, and both sides to the top of the cap, and the center of the crown to be embroidered with the same number of braids.
For enlisted men the cap will be of the same pattern; the band to be dark blue, and, as in the case of officers, the several arms of service will be designated by the color of the sides and crown—red for artillery, light blue for infantry, and yellow for cavalry. The number of the regiment will be worn in front in yellow metal.
  In hot weather a white duck or linen cover, known as a havelock, will be worn—the apron to fall behind, so as to protect the ears and neck from the rays of the sun. In winter in bad weather an oilskin cover will be worn, with an apron to fall over the coat collar.

By command of the
Secretary of War
S. Cooper

Adjutant and Inspector General
Later, regulations for C. S. surgeons were explicitly laid down as follows:

Gray frock coat with black collar and cuffs, green silk net sash, dark blue trousers with a black stripe 1¼ inches wide piped with gold. The hat was a gold-edged, black cocked hat.

Although the Southern uniform was supposed to be gray, the soldiers wore homespun of all colors. There was no regular supply of overcoats. Woolen shirts and socks were very scarce. The excellent double-thick overcoat of the Federal soldier was usually warmer than every article of clothing which the Southern soldier had combined. A Confederate soldier, H. V. Redfield of Tennessee, believed that the C. S. Government never even attempted to issue overcoats to their men; at least, he never saw any two overcoats the same during his entire service throughout the war.

So far as other items of clothing were concerned, Confederate soldiers wore out their jackets in three months—their trousers in one month. Sometimes the men wore cotton trousers in winter because wool and flannel was almost impossible to get. Shoes were scarce everywhere after early 1862.

In January 1862, the clothing bureau of the Confederate War Department had 100,000 complete uniforms on hand. The donations of individual states to their own volunteers had substantially lessened the demand for uniforms from the C. S. Government.

But soon improvisation and make-do were the order of the day. Blankets were shipped to Richmond to be made into overcoats. As early as 1862, a Mrs. E. H. Chamberlain of Edgefield District in South Carolina was making clothing in two unique ways: with the warp of cotton—the filling of rabbit fur; and also with cotton warp but with the filling of coon fur. In Savannah, Georgia, a public collection was made in October 1862 of carpets to be made into uniforms. Enough was collected to make over 500 blankets in addition to the uniforms.

In addition to these many improvisations, the Confederate soldier did not hesitate to

"I can only say he is a Confederate gray" —Lee on "Traveller." (Courtesy *Photographic History of the Civil War*) This famous photograph of Lee on "Traveller" was taken by Miley, of Lexington, in September 1866.

use captured Federal items. Many wagon loads of Federal uniforms and clothing from the discards made during a long march were picked up by green troops or any troops at the beginning of spring campaigning. These items, usually picked up and loaded in wagons by local civilians, consisted of overcoats, blankets, dress coats, and vests. Occasionally, the men even threw away caps, boots, socks, shirts, and drawers. All these items were either hidden by the civilians in their houses and barns or were sent to help clothe the ill-clad soldiers of the Confederate armies. And thus the clothing accounts of many of the Federal troops were often unwittingly duplicated for the benefit of the men they were fighting. From this source, and from what was taken from Federals who were taken prisoner, and from what was gained by stripping the dead and wounded left on the field, the Confederate soldiers received a large share of their clothing.

The newspaper reporter Henry Villard (New York *Herald*), at Fort Donelson noted that the great majority of Confederate captured there "were only partially uniformed, or were wholly in civilian clothes and presented a very motley, dirty, and anything but respect-inspiring appearance."

COLOR OF UNIFORM

Although gray was the officially adopted color for Confederate Army uniforms, the color known as "butternut" was worn very extensively. A good description of the preparation of "butternut" coloring was provided by a soldier of the 1st Iowa Infantry.

In Missouri, the women carded wool and cotton together and spun it into yarn. Then they dyed the yarn with walnut or butternut bark; it was all called "butternut"; then it was woven on home-made looms into cloth. The cloth was then dyed again, and became a reddish brown. This cloth was firm and desirable. Any carpenter could make a loom and any woman could operate it. We saw many looms in operation during the campaign [1861], and in every house were the cards to card the wool and cotton and the wheels to spin them. The war put indigo out of the market, and "butternut" remained abundant—therefore Confederate uniform for Missouri and Arkansas troops became "butternut." Up North the Copperheads adopted it; they cross-sliced butternuts and polished the slices, then wore them as buttons, scarf pins, and jewelry. When the 1st Iowa Infantry returned home in September 1861, they went around in squads and hunted for people who wore butternuts and took them off.

Hundreds of Confederate dead at South Mountain (September 14, 1862) were dressed in coarse butternut-colored uniforms, "very ugly in appearance but admirably well calculated to conceal them from our troops."

Cadet of the Virginia Military Institute in marching outfit—a sketch. U.S. Signal Corps photo, Brady Collection. (Courtesy The National Archives)

SPECIAL UNIFORMS

While regulations specified the uniform for all Confederate soldiers, many state volunteer and militia units wore uniforms of their own design. This was most obvious in the designs of buttons, belt buckles, and cartridge box plates. However, even individuals often wore their own outfits. For example, a Confederate officer in Tennessee wore a gray uniform and a moose-colored slouch hat with a black plume, with a white cotton handkerchief tied under his chin.

Some units, such as the "Rockbridge Dragoons" (Co. "H" 14th Virginia Cavalry), went to war wearing leather helmets, probably dating back to the War of 1812 era. Other Southerners wore the "Corsican" cap, a forage cap with bag and tassel hanging down the left side of the head.

Some of the distinctive uniforms were worn by the following units:

VIRGINIA

1st Virginia Infantry

Apparently each company of this regiment had its own distinctive uniform. Field officers wore a blue coat and trousers, Virginia buttons, and the Jeff Davis hat.

"Virginia Life Guard" (Company "B" 15th Virginia Infantry)

The uniforms for this regiment were made by the Crenshaw Woolen Mills of Richmond, Virginia. The uniform consisted of blue flannel cloth hunting shirts with blue fringe, Virginia buttons, blue cloth cap, black pants, and white gloves.

Virginia Military Institute (VMI)

In 1864, when VMI cadets fought at Newmarket, Virginia, they wore a coarse sheep's-gray jacket and trousers. The jacket had seven buttons and a plain black tape stripe. The cap was of the simple forage type.

"Black Horse Cavalry" (1st Virginia Cavalry)

The uniform was gray or butternut, but also with much color variation throughout the regiment. Officers wore a braided coat. The hat was wide-brimmed with a plume. Enlisted men wore light jackets, trousers with black facings, slouch hats (often decorated with plumes). Material used in these uniforms was homespun.

ALABAMA

1st Alabama Infantry

In March 1862, while still in Montgomery, Alabama, men of the 1st Alabama Infantry were issued enameled cloth knapsacks and haversacks as well as cedar canteens, but they provided their own uniforms, *no two of which were alike.*

Alabama Volunteer Cadets

In a letter dated September 6, 1861, Sergeant Fred C. Floyd of the 40th New York Infantry described meeting Confederate pickets near Alexandria, Virginia. These pickets wore caps decorated with the letters *A.V.C.* —standing for Alabama Volunteer Cadets.

LOUISIANA

Louisiana Zouaves

This flashy outfit wore a jacket decoratel with braid of various colors, blue shirt, scarlet Zouave pants, large blue sash, white gaiters, and a fez.

SOUTH CAROLINA

As in other Southern states the volunteer companies chose their own uniforms and they did so. However, most of them wore the palmetto insignia. There was an endless variety to the uniforms worn. Some men wore a gray coat trimmed with green, white trousers, and black hat.

Coats were of different colors, designs, and materials. The most common colors were gray, green, and blue—all combined with such colors as yellow or orange. Some of the materials used were linen, flannel, and tweed. Headgear were generally kepis, but some men wore leather helmets, either the crested dragoon type or the Prussian spike type.

Illustrative of an early South Carolina uniform was that worn by some officers in Charleston in mid-April 1861. They wore blue caps with the palmetto insignia, blue coats with upright collars, shoulder straps, gilt buttons with the palmetto in relief, and blue trousers with a gold lace cord.

The British war correspondent William Howard Russell, on April 12, 1861, in commenting on the uniforms, wrote:

There is an endless variety—often of ugliness—in dress and equipment and nomenclature among these companies. The headdress is generally, however, a smart cap like the French kepi; the tunic is of different cuts, colors, facings, and materials—green

General Joseph E. Johnson, C.S.A. (Courtesy *Civil War Times Illustrated*)

Confederate cavalry: Mosby and Confederate partisans. (Courtesy *Civil War Times Illustrated*)

with gray and yellow, gray with orange and black and white, blue with white and yellow facings, roan, brown, burnt sienna and olive—jackets, frocks, tunics, blouses, cloth, linen, tweed, flannel.

It is interesting to note that in all Southern states in 1861, officers of the "old army" (i.e., United States Army) wore their blue uniforms until they could purchase the new gray. South Carolina officers continued to wear the "old army" blue for several months after the outbreak of war.

States like Georgia and North Carolina, in early 1861, wore uniforms much similar to the regulation Federal uniform. These Southerners wore a dark blue uniform but with appropriate State insignia replacing the United States insignia.

NEGRO UNIT

The Charleston *Evening News* of May 1, 1861, described the arrival in Petersburg, Virginia of 125 free Negroes, uniformed with red shirts and dark pants, bearing the flag of the Confederacy. They were to work on the fortifications around Norfolk. These men "were all in the finest spirits, and seemed anxious to 'catch Old Linkum one time' . . . They certainly deserve great credit for their disinterestedness, and find that it is appreciated."

SHOES

Confederate soldiers got their shoes from various sources. Early in the war many pairs were shipped from overseas through the Federal blockade. For example, the blockade runner *Antonica* in January 1863 included in its manifest a valuable cargo of army shoes and other items. The *Antonica* and several other ships were due to leave Nassau early in 1863 with similar "valuable cargoes" for the Confederacy.

Another source was from the enemy. It was a custom among the poorly shod Confederate troops to remove shoes from dead Federal soldiers after a battle. This was not done in any spirit of vandalism or heartlessness. The shoes were taken off to supply men who had much marching to do in inclement weather. The Confederate soldier merely exchanged old, worn-out shoes for good ones on the feet of men who would have no further use for them. Also, it was common practice for Confederates to exchange their worn-out footwear with the superior shoes or boots

Louisiana "Pelican." U.S. Signal Corps photo, Brady Collection. (Courtesy The National Archives)

of Federal officers and men whom they captured.

In the last analysis, however, the Confederacy was to be dependent primarily on its own shoe-producing facilities. Up to 1861, the South had purchased large quantities of leather goods from the North. Of course this supply was cut off by the war. But soldiers, and civilians as well, needed shoes. How were they to be supplied?

General P. G. T. Beauregard, C.S.A. U.S.
Signal Corps photo, Brady Collection.
(Courtesy The National Archives)

General Robert E. Lee. U.S. Signal Corps photo, Brady Collection. (Courtesy The National Archives)

Several Southern states had reserve supplies of leather at the outbreak of war. Alabama, for example, was in good leather supply. The Alabama press urged that a company be organized to buy up hides throughout the state and make them into shoes. In 1861,

Alabama had enough shoe factories to do this. In late 1861, Mr. Charles B. May opened a patent-leather factory in Montgomery, Alabama, assisted by three workmen from the North.

By January 1862, the Southern shoe manufacturers were saying that overproduction was prevalent in the shoe business. At this time the Confederate Government had 600 cases of army shoes more than was needed, while contractors were supplying 200 pairs a day.

But as the war went on this situation changed drastically. Soon the South was seeking leather substitutes for making shoes. Shoes were made of felt with wax and rosin. Old saddle skirts and leather ginbands were used. Even shoes were made of leather or felt with such wood as white oak, hickory, palmetto stalk, or birch in between. Attempts were made in Florida to gather and cure the weed "kip leather" to make shoes, which shoemakers claimed to be equal to the best French leather. Such leather had been prepared by Isaac Bierfield of Newberry, South Carolina, who had a patent on the process. On January 1, 1862, the Raleigh, North Carolina, *Standard* described the wooden-shoe factory of Thuim and Fraps of Raleigh. This factory made shoes of gumwood and poplar. The shoes were topped with leather and were of lighter weight than all-leather shoes. This factory produced 100 pairs of shoes daily.

BUTTONS

In addition to the buttons prescribed by regulations, buttons with the letters "CSA"— State Coat of Arms, or the initials of volunteer and militia units were also extensively worn. Sergeant Fred C. Floyd of the 40th New York Infantry noted that Confederates captured at Williamsburg wore uniforms of varying colors. Prisoners from South Carolina wore uniforms whose buttons had a palmetto tree with the motto *Anima opibusque parati,* which translated reads: "Prepared in mind and resources." Sergeant Floyd asked one of the prisoners the meaning of the motto—and received the quick reply: "Give the damn Yankees fits."

During the war, under the caption "A Premium Uniform," Richmond newspapers published the following interesting incident:

Recently Mrs. White of Selma, Alabama, went through the lines to Lexington, Kentucky, and being a sister (Todd) of Mrs. Lincoln, was permitted to go on to Washington. On her return, several weeks ago, she was allowed to carrying nothing back, save a uniform for a very dear friend of hers who was battling in the Southern cause. The uniform arrived in the Confederacy several days since, and on inspection all the buttons were found to be composed of gold coin—two and a half, five, ten, and twenty-dollar gold pieces, set in the wooden button and covered with Confederate cloth. The gold thus brought through is valued at between thirty and forty thousand dollars— all sewed upon a uniform.

BUCKLES

Confederate buckles varied greatly in shape and design. In addition to the letters C.S.A. or C.S., the various states were often represented by belt buckles with the state seal or initials on them.

CONFEDERATE STATES NAVY

(From *Uniform and Dress of the Navy of the Confederate States*)

Undress: [Sea Officers] Coat

For a Flag Officer, shall be a frockcoat of steel-gray cloth, faced with the same and lined with black silk serge, double breasted, with two rows of large navy buttons on the breast, nine in each row, placed four inches and a half apart from eye to eye at top, and two inches and a half at bottom. Rolling collar, skirts to be full, commencing at the top of the hip bone and descending four-fifths thence towards the knee, with one button behind on each hip and one near the bottom of each fold. The cuffs to be two inches and a half deep, with one strip of gold lace one-half an inch wide below the seam, but joining it;

C. R. M. Pohlé of Richmond, Virginia,
drum-major of the crack Richmond regiment, the First Virginia, as photographed
in April 1861. (Courtesy Library of Congress)

Charles F. Mosby, a Confederate drummer boy who enlisted at the age of 13 and served from 1861 to 1865 throughout the war, first with the "Elliott Grays" of the Sixth Virginia Infantry and later with Henderson's heavy artillery. (Courtesy Library of Congress)

three strips of lace of the same width on the sleeves above the cuffs, separated by a space of three-eighths of an inch from each other, the upper one with a loop three inches long, and a strip of lace half an inch wide, from the lower button to the end of the cuffs on the upper side of the opening, and four small-sized buttons (navy buttons) in the opening.

For a Captain, the same as for a Flag Offi-cer, except that there shall be but three strips of lace around the sleeve and cuff, including the looped strip.

For a Commander, the same in all respects as for a Captain, except that there shall be but two strips of lace around the sleeve and cuff, including the looped strip, and three small buttons in the opening.

For a Lieutenant, the same in all respects

as for a Commander, except that the cuffs shall have but one strip of gold lace, looped, around the upper edge.

For a Master, the same as for a Lieutenant, except that the cuffs shall have but one strip of lace one-fourth of an inch wide, without a loop, around the upper edge.

For a Passed Midshipman, the same as for a Master, excepting that the cuffs shall have, instead of lace, three medium-sized navy buttons around the upper edge.

For a Midshipman, the same as for a Passed Midshipman, except that medium sized buttons shall be substituted for the large buttons.

Undress [Civil officers] Coat

For a Surgeon of over twelve years' standing, shall be a frock coat of steel gray cloth, faced with the same, double breasted, rolling collar, with two rows of large navy buttons on the breast, nine in each row, proportion for body and skirts the same as for a captain, skirts lined with black silk serge, one button behind on each hip, and one near the bottom of each fold of the skirts. Cuffs the same as for a commander, except that a plain strip of

Charleston Zouaves. (Courtesy Library of Congress)

123

lace shall be substituted for the loop.

For a Surgeon of less than twelve years' standing, the same, except that there shall be one strip of lace around the cuff and sleeve.

For a Passed Assistant Surgeon the same as for a Surgeon of less than twelve years' standing, except that the lace on the cuff shall be one-quarter of an inch wide.

For an Assistant Surgeon, the same as for a Surgeon, except that instead of lace there shall be three medium sized buttons on the cuff.

For a Paymaster of over twelve years' standing, the same as prescribed for a Surgeon over twelve years.

For a Paymaster of less than twelve years' standing, the same as for a Surgeon of less than twelve years.

For a Chief Engineer of more than twelve years' standing, the same as for a Surgeon of more than twelve years.

For a First Assistant Engineer, the same as for a Chief Engineer, except that there shall be but one strip of lace on the cuff one-quarter of an inch wide.

For a Second and Third Assistant, the same as for a First Assistant Engineer, except that instead of lace the cuffs shall have three medium sized buttons around the upper edge.

For a Chaplain, the same as for a Surgeon, except that it shall be single breasted, with one row of nine large navy buttons on the breast. The cuffs plain with three small buttons in the opening.

For a Professor and Commodore's Secretary, the same as for a Chaplain, except that there shall be but eight buttons on the breast.

For a Clerk, the same as for a Secretary, except that there shall be but six buttons on the breast.

Vest

For all officers, steel gray or white, single breasted, standing collar, with nine small buttons in front, and not to show below the coat.

Pantaloons

For all officers, shall be of steel gray cloth or white drill, made loose to spread well over the foot and to be worn over boots or shoes.

Shoulder Straps

For a Flag Officer, of sky-blue cloth, edged with black, four inches long and one inch and three-eighths wide, bordered with an embroidery of gold one-quarter of an inch in width, with four stars in line at equal distances, the two on the ends six-tenths of an inch in diameter, and the two intermediate six-eighths of an inch in diameter.

For a Captain, the same as for a Flag Officer, except that there shall be three stars at equal distances, each six-tenths of an inch in diameter.

For a Commander, the same as for a Captain, except that there shall be but two stars.

For a Lieutenant, the same as for a Commander, except that there shall be but one star, in the centre.

For a Master, the same as for a Lieutenant, except that there shall be no star.

For a Passed Midshipman, a strip of gold lace four inches long and half an inch wide.

For a Surgeon of more than twelve years' standing, the same as for a Master, except that they shall be of black cloth, with two sprigs of olive, crossed, embroidered in gold in the centre.

For a Surgeon of less than twelve years' standing, the same except that there shall be but one sprig of olive.

For a passed Assistant Surgeon, the same as for a Surgeon, except that instead of sprigs of olive, there shall be an olive leaf embroidered in gold on each end.

For an Assistant Surgeon, the same as for a Passed Assistant Surgeon, without the leaves.

For a Paymaster, of more than twelve years' standing, the same as for a Surgeon of more than twelve years, except that the straps shall be of dark green cloth.

Confederate bandsmen. (Courtesy Moravian Music Foundation, Salem, N.C.)

For a Paymaster, of less than twelve years' standing, the same as for a Surgeon of less than twelve years, except that the straps shall be of dark green cloth.

For an Assistant Paymaster, the same as for an Assistant Surgeon, except that the straps shall be of dark green cloth.

For a Chief Engineer of more than twelve years' standing, the same as for a Master, except that there shall be two sprigs of live oak embroidered in gold in the centre, and the straps shall be of dark blue cloth.

For a Chief Engineer of less than twelve years' standing, the same, except that there shall be but one sprig of live oak.

Caps

Cap of steel-gray cloth, to be not less than three inches and a half, nor more than four inches in height, and not more than ten nor less than nine inches and a half at top, with patent leather visor, to be worn by all officers in service dress.

For a Flag Officer, the device shall be a foul anchor in an open wreath of live oak leaves, with four stars above the anchor, embroi-

dered in gold as per pattern, on the front of the cap above a band of gold lace one inch and three quarters wide.

For a Captain, the same as for a flag officer, except that there shall be but three stars above the anchor, and the gold band shall be one and one half inches wide.

For a Commander, the same as for a Captain, except that there shall be but two stars.

For a Lieutenant, the same as for a Commander, except that there shall be but one star.

For a Master, the same as for a Lieutenant, except that there shall be no star.

For a Passed Midshipman, a foul anchor without the wreath.

For a Surgeon, of over twelve years' standing, a wreath of olive leaves with three stars, four tenths of an inch in diameter, embroidered in gold as per pattern, on the front of the cap, above a band of gold lace one inch and a quarter wide.

For a Surgeon, of less than twelve years' standing, the same, except that there shall be two stars.

For a Passed Assistant Surgeon, the same

125

Major Israel Greene, C.S. Marine Corps. This officer commanded a detachment of U.S. Marines sent to Harpers Ferry in 1859 to capture John Brown. Greene resigned from the U.S. Marine Corps at the outbreak of war to enter the Confederate Marine Corps. Defense Dept. photo (Marine Corps)

as for a Surgeon, except that there shall be but one star.

For an Assistant Surgeon, the same as for a Surgeon, except that there shall be no star.

For a Paymaster, of over twelve years' standing, the same as for a Surgeon of over twelve years' standing.

For a Paymaster, of less than twelve years, the same as for a Surgeon of less than twelve years.

For an Assistant Paymaster, the same as for an Assistant Surgeon.

For a Chief Engineer, of more than twelve years' standing, the same as for a Surgeon of more than twelve years, except that the letter E in old English character shall be embroidered in gold below the stars.

For a Chief Engineer, of less than twelve years, the same, except that there shall be but two stars.

For Second and Third Assistant Engineers, the same as for a First Assistant Engineer, except that there shall be no stars.

Buttons

Buttons shall be of three sizes: large, medium, and small, and all of the same device, as per pattern.

Summer Frockcoat

In summer or in tropical climates, officers may wear frockcoats and pantaloons of steel-gray summer cloth of the style and pattern herein prescribed, with medium-size navy buttons.

Jackets

May be worn as service dress by all officers when at sea, except when at general muster. To be of steel gray cloth or white drill linen with the same, double breasted, rolling collar, same number of small sized buttons on breast as for undress coat, open fly sleeve with four small buttons in the opening, with shoulder straps for appropriate grades.

Straw Hats

In summer or in tropical climates, officers may also wear, except at general muster, white straw hats. The body of the hat to be six inches in height, and the rim three and a half inches in width.

Overcoats

For all officers, shall be of steel gray cloth, double breasted, rolling collar, skirts to descend three inches below the knee, the same number of navy buttons, and similarly arranged as for undress coat. No buttons to be worn on the cuffs or pocket flaps. Officers entitled to shoulder straps will wear the same on their overcoats as directed for undress coats. Gray cloth cloaks may be worn in boats.

Dress for Petty Officers and Crew

Boatswain's Mates, Gunner's Mates, Carpenter's Mates, Sailmaker's Mates, Ship's Steward and Ship's Cook, will wear embroidered in black silk on the right sleeve of their gray jackets above the elbow in front, a foul anchor of not more than three inches length. The same device embroidered blue to be worn on the sleeves of their white frocks in summer.

All other petty officers except officers, stewards and yeomen will wear the same device on their left sleeve.

The outside clothing for petty officers, firemen and coal-heavers, seamen, ordinary seamen, landsmen and boys for muster, shall consist of gray cloth jackets and trousers, or gray woolen frocks with white duck cuffs and collars, black hats, black silk neckerchiefs and shoes, or boots in cold weather. In warm weather it shall consist of white frocks and trousers, black or white hats, as the commander may for the occasion direct, having proper regard for the comfort of the crew; black silk neckerchiefs and shoes. The collars and cuffs to be lined with blue cotton cloth, and stitched round with thread. Thick gray caps without visors may be worn by the crew at sea, except on holidays or at muster.

For a Boatswain, Gunner, Carpenter and Sailmaker, shall be of steel gray cloth, lined with the same; rolling collar, double breasted, two rows of large navy buttons on the breast, eight in each row; pointed pocket flaps, with three large buttons underneath each, showing one-half their diameter; three medium size buttons around each cuff, and two small ones in each opening; one button behind on each hip; one in the middle of each fold, and one in each fold near the bottom of the skirt. On each side of the collar to have one loop of three-quarters wide gold lace, to show one inch and a half wide, and four inches long, with a small size navy button in the point of each loop.

CONFEDERATE PRIVATEERS

On April 17, 1861, the President of the

Lieutenant Francis H. Cameron, C.S. Marine Corps. (Courtesy Lee Wallace, Jr.)

Confederate States of America issued a proclamation inviting "all those who may desire" to aid the Confederate cause by service in "private armed vessels." Interested persons were instructed to make application for commissions or "letters of marque and reprisal" to be issued under the seal of the Cenfederate States. Each person applying was told to furnish a statement in writing giving the name, description, tonnage of the vessel he would furnish and the *intended number of the crew.* Nothing was said about uniform of the crew members since they remained civilians, although often the officers were duly commissioned Confederate States naval personnel. However, officers and crew members were subject to the laws of the Confederate States.

The wisdom of not issuing uniforms to privateer crew members is readily seen when one realizes that on such ships as the *Alabama,* the crew was made up of British subjects.

CONFEDERATE STATES MARINE CORPS

The author is indebted to the noted Civil War authority Lee A. Wallace, Jr., for much of the following data, and for the illustrations of Confederate marine officers.)

Material on uniforms of the C. S. Marine Corps is extremely fragmentary. Apparently the uniform was gray, but otherwise varied considerably in design with individuals. This lack of uniformity is readily apparent in the accompanying illustrations. Caps were worn and different weight cloth was used for cold weather and hot weather. Some officers wore shoulder straps to designate rank, while other officers wore woven sleeve braid for the same purpose.

Unlike the Confederate Army and Navy, no detailed description of the uniform for the C. S. Marine Corps is known to exist. It is known that gray was the prescribed color, and from various sources it has been possible to get a fair picture of the uniform worn by

Confederate marines. It is quite likely that the prescribed uniform was patterned after that worn at that time by the U.S. Marine Corps, with the substitution of gray for blue.

Officers

A photograph of 2nd Lieutenant Henry M. Doak, C.S. Marine Corps, taken after July 7, 1862, shows him wearing a double-breasted frockcoat which was undoubtedly gray. Seven buttons appear on each row. Rank is indicated by a single bar on each side of the collar, and sleeve braid, in the same manner as prescribed for the C.S. Army. Doak is wearing a sword belt but the belt plate does not appear distinct enough to detect size, shape, or design. A white collar appears well above the collar. He is holding a foreign-type cap by its visor, but no further details of the cap are visible. Gray cloth caps are known to

Confederate hat wreath, actual size. Brass-stamped with lead-filled back.

have been worn by C. S. Marine Corps officers. The uniform of Lt. Francis H. Cameron, shown here, consists of a double-breasted frockcoat with a fairly high turndown, or roll, collar showing above it. The coat appears to be blue, or perhaps black alpaca. The sleeve braid denoting rank is the army pattern.

Both blue and gray trousers were worn by officers of the C. S. Marine Corps.

Enlisted Men

Headgear: Felt hat similar to one worn by other privates.

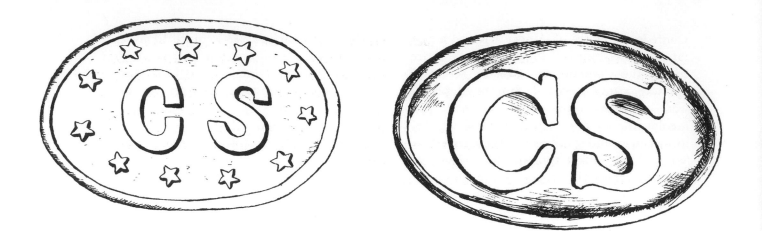

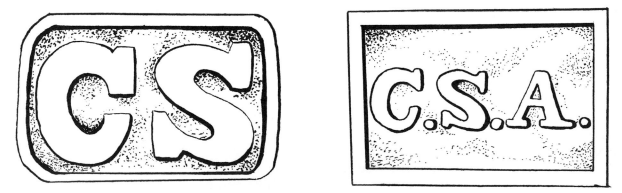

Types of Confederate belt plates. (Courtesy Mike McAfee)

Shirt: Blue flannel shirt, probably pullover type with four white buttons.

Trousers: Sky-blue kersey trousers of the same cut as worn by the U.S. Marine Corps as per regulations of 1859.

On May 6, 1861 Captain Alfred C. Van Benthuysen's company of Marines stationed at Pensacola, Florida, wore blue pants and gray flannel shirts. Later in 1861 the men received white pants, blue flannel shirts, and white shirts or jumpers. The articles of clothing just described were probably intended only as temporary dress until a regulation uniform could be provided. This regulation uniform was probably of the same pattern as worn by the U.S. Marines, but was gray in color.

6

Prisoners, Bushwhackers, Deserters, Veterans

UNIFORMS FOR U.S. PRISONERS

By laws of the Confederacy, Federal prisoners of war had to be furnished with clothing. However, the Confederacy never made arrangements to issue this clothing, and never did issue any clothing to the prisoners in its prison camps. As a result, prisoners in Libby and elsewhere reported that they were suffering, even dying from exposure because of the lack of sufficient clothing. Headgear, shirts, overcoats, socks, and shoes were lacking and even officers slept on bare floors with no covers. The Confederates claimed they didn't have clothing to give Federal prisoners in their prison camps but were perfectly willing to allow friends of the Federal prisoners to send clothing to them.

Federal prisoners who enlisted in the Confederate service wore the uniform of the Confederacy. In November 1864, escaped Federal officers reported to General H. W. Halleck that between 1,300 and 2,000 Federal soldiers had taken the oath of allegiance to the Confederacy. These men were clothed in the C.S. Army uniform.

UNIFORMS FOR C.S. PRISONERS

Confederate prisoners wore the uniforms in which they were captured during their stay in Federal prisoner of war camps. As these uniforms wore out the men were issued plain "prison garb." At one of the largest Federal prisons for Confederates (Elmira, New York), the prison commandant was sharply rebuked by General W. Hoffman (Federal Commissary-General of Prisoners) for not furnishing the Confederate prisoners with prison garb, but issuing United States uniforms instead.

On February 15, 1865, General H. W. Halleck, Chief of Staff, informed Grant that 1,000 bales of cotton were being sold in order to supply Confederate prisoners, soon to be exchanged, with new uniforms and blankets. Thus, they would return to the battle front in uniforms furnished by the United States. This had been accomplished by a contract of the C.S. General Wm. N. R. Beall in New York for 20,000 gray uniforms. These uniforms conformed completely to C.S. regulations except for the buttons.

General Beall was a paroled prisoner and personally visited Boston, Philadelphia, Baltimore, and New York City, where he also purchased blankets, socks, underwear, shirts, and shoes for the Confederate prisoners.

In reply to this letter, Grant suggested that the Federals exchange prisoners who had not

Culpeper Court House, Virginia, August
1862. A group of Confederate soldiers on
the balcony of the court house, captured
at Cedar Mt. Photo by T. H. O'Sullivan.
(Courtesy Library of Congress)

been outfitted by General Beall's purchases. In this way, the newly uniformed Confederates would keep their uniforms but could only wear them in prison since they would not be exchanged.

However, it was soon learned that the arrangements for exchange of the newly uniformed Confederate prisoners were too far advanced and it was not possible to prevent their return to the Confederate lines.

The general policy of Commissary General of Prisoners Hoffman was to issue only cloth-ing needed for immediate use. And these clothes were to be of such quality which would not last very long after the prisoner's exchange. If prisoners bought boots, these too were to be of poor quality. Prisoners were not permitted to buy items of uniform.

In January 1862, Hoffman was ordered to issue to prisoners of war only defective cloth-ing which had been rejected as unfit for Federal military use.

In July 1863, Hoffman informed the Federal prison commandant that Confederate prisoners were limited to one suit and a change of underclothing. If prisoners wished to buy clothing, the suits must be of gray cloth with plain buttons and no trimming. Shoes must still be of poor quality and now boots were forbidden altogether.

CONFEDERATES IN U.S. ARMY UNIFORMS AS "GALVANIZED YANKEES"

A few thousand Confederate prisoners of war enlisted in the United States service during the war to get away from tedious and often unhealthy prison life. Some of these men, known as "Galvanized Yankees," were organized into regiments and were sent West to fight the Indians. The exact number of "Galvanized Yankees" will never be known. It is known that some enlisted in the Federal Navy and such regiments as the 2nd New Hampshire Infantry where they fought well. The uniforms worn by ex-Confederate prisoners of war were those of the Federal unit in which the Southerners served.

Sudley Ford, Bull Run, March 1862. Photo by C. M. Barnard. (Courtesy Library of Congress)

134

AS SPIES AND GUERRILLAS

Confederate soldiers, by necessity, wore captured Federal items of uniform, especially the less conspicuous articles of clothing, such as shirts, underwear, socks and shoes. The stripping of dead Federals of their shoes was common practice. Also widely worn were Federal overcoats and raincoats, and even other articles such as jackets and trousers. Whenever possible, the strictly military parts of the uniform were dyed gray or butternut.

This appropriation and use by the Confederates of essential clothing items was understood by Federals to be inevitable and justifiable. But the Confederate use of Federal uniforms by spies or guerrillas was the cause of much bitterness and a series of military laws condemning such practice. The first of these was prepared by Francis Lieber in his epochal *Instructions for the Government of the United States in the Field.* Issued as General Orders No. 100, Adjutant General's Office, April 24, 1863, the United States stated its policy as follows:

Section 63: Troops who fight in the uniform of their enemies, without any plain, striking, and uniform mark of distinction of their own, can expect no quarter.
Section 64: If American troops capture a train containing uniforms of the enemy, and the commander considers it advisable to distribute them for use among his men, some striking mark or sign must be adopted to distinguish the American soldier from the enemy.

The issuance of this order had been triggered by several incidents involving Confederate use of Federal uniforms in both major theaters of the war. Federal commanders had tended to write their own laws. On January 26, 1863, by General Orders No. 10, Department of the Tennessee, General U. S. Grant had ordered that:

guerrillas or Southern soldiers caught in the uniforms of Federal soldiers would not be treated as organized bodies of the enemy but would be closely confined and held for the action of the War Department. Those caught within the lines of the Federal Army in such uniforms or in civilian clothing would be treated as spies.

And in the East the Federal commander of the Department of Maryland on March 29, 1863, had ordered that any officer or soldier of the Confederate Army found within Federal lines wearing clothing or accouterments of the U.S. would be dealt with as a spy. The Confederate authorities had promptly replied that articles of clothing and accouterments were legitimate objects of capture under the rules of war and may be used by the captors.

Francis Lieber's well-considered statement of United States policy had little immediate effect on the Confederates. Only four days after the issuance of the famous General Orders No. 100 (i.e. on April 28, 1863), the commander of the 8th Missouri Cavalry (Federal) reported that seven of his men were murdered by "rebels dressed in Federal uniform . . . [who] rode up to them as friends," stripped and murdered them, and threw them into a heap "like so many hogs."

On August 30, 1863, Sherman wrote Grant at Vicksburg that two men, professing to belong to Pinson's cavalry had been captured wearing no uniform, no marks of a soldier's dress, not even dressed alike." Both wore civilian clothing and Sherman said that the Federals should insist that their enemy wear a uniform—"something to distinguish them from the common citizen." Sherman asked if they should not be treated as spies, since they were fully equipped and were dogging a Federal mounted patrol. Grant ordered the men to be confined in a jail until he could communicate with his superiors.

Because the Confederates continued the practice of wearing captured Federal uniforms, the United States military commanders began to treat as spies any Confederates captured in Federal uniform. On January 5, 1864, by General Orders No. 3, Department of the Ohio, Private E. S. Dodd, 8th Texas Cavalry, was executed as a spy. He was caught wearing the U.S. uniform. As a result of his case, the commander of the Department of the Ohio issued General Orders No. 7 (January 8, 1864) directing corps commanders to execute by firing squad "all the rebel officers and soldiers wearing the uniform of the U.S. Army" who might be captured within the Federal lines.

The Confederates took strong exception to such Federal action. On February 3, 1864, Colonel T. R. Freeman, C.S. Army, Camp Ferguson, Arkansas, pointed out that hundreds of Confederates were captured wearing Federal uniforms and were later exchanged without incurring punishment by their Federal captors. "Besides, the laws of war have always allowed one army to deceive another either by wearing the enemy's uniform or hoisting its flag."

Apparently, the Federal high command refused to back up the strong measures requested by commanders in the field. For example, the commander of the Cavalry Corps, Army of the Potomac on January 15, 1864, ordered that "every guerrilla or other rebel" wearing the uniform of a U. S. soldier, caught in the act of making war against Federal forces would be hanged. But this order was revoked by higher authority on April 5, 1864. No reason for this revocation was given.

BUSHWHACKERS

An officer (Captain Charles Leib) described bushwhackers whom he saw in western Virginia in 1861-1862. His description would apply to bushwhackers on both sides and in all areas of the border States.

Imagine a stolid, vicious-looking countenance, an ungainly figure (clothed) in a garb of the coarsest texture of homespun linen or linsey-woolsey, tattered and torn, and so covered with dirt as not to enable one to guess its original color; a dilapidated, rimless hat or cap of some wild animal covering his head, which has not been combed for months; his feet covered with moccasins, and a rifle by his side, a powder horn and a shot-pouch slung around his neck . . . Thus equipped, he sallies forth with the stealth of the panther, and lies in wait for a straggling soldier . . . to whom the only warning given of his presence is the sharp click of his deadly rifle.

Uniform for Slackers

A cartoon in *Harper's Weekly* for September 7, 1861, suggested a "Costume . . . for the Brave Stay-at-Home 'Light Guards' " to consist of a broom, dust pan and feather duster for weapons, a saucepan for a hat, and stays and hoop skirts for uniforms!

Sale of Uniforms by Deserters

In General Orders No. 122, September 11, 1863, the Confederate military authorities called attention to the Confederate Congress act which provided that:

Every person, not subject to the Rules and Articles of War, who shall procure or entice a soldier of the Confederate States to desert, or who shall purchase from any soldier his arms, uniform, clothing, or any part thereof . . . shall be fined . . . in any sum not exceeding three hundred dollars and be imprisoned not exceeding one year.

DISCHARGED VETERANS

Considerable confusion exists as to the number of genuine Confederate uniforms which survived the war. Only a comparatively few lasted until 1865, and *very* few of them are still in existence. Most of the so-called "Confederate uniforms" in collections today are postwar gray uniforms made for such veterans' organizations as the United Confederate Veterans (UCV). In some cases,

Confederate uniform in the field; three Confederate soldiers captured at Gettysburg. Note the plain uniforms and typical "rebel slouch hat." (Courtesy Library of Congress)

original gray Confederate cloth was made into uniforms *after* the war for sentimental reasons. The original Confederate uniforms, worn during the war, were worn out by their wearers because no civilian clothing was available.

Many Confederate soldiers, returning home at the war's end, only had their military uniforms as clothing which they could wear. But some Federal military authorities con-sidered it ill-advised to permit the late enemy to continue to parade the uniform of the Confederacy. Accordingly, local regulations were laid down by Federal commanders restricting the wearing of the Confederate uniform. In Savannah, Georgia, large numbers of Confederate officers came in and gave themselves up to Federal troops garrisoning the city. These officers were paroled, and allowed to wear their uniforms—most of them

The Gray and the Blue—Lt. James B. Washington, C.S.A., a prisoner (left) and Lt. George A. Custer, U.S.A., in May 1862. Photo by J. F. Gibson. (Courtesy Library of Congress)

had no other clothes—but every military insignia had to be removed—particularly the brass buttons were all cut from their coats. To this proceeding some of them angrily refused, but the Federal officers were inexorable. At one time a captain of the 14th New Hampshire Infantry had a dozen of these officers before him. When he proceeded to dispossess them of the buttons with C.S.A. on them, the officers refused to be shorn. When notified that it was a matter of minus buttons or minus freedom, they agreed to cut them off if left to themselves. They were gratified, and went off wearing buttonless coats.

However, in the Department of the Gulf, General N. P. Banks in General Orders No. 47, April 30, 1865, decreed that no paroled prisoners of war in the Department could appear in public in "the uniform of the rebel army."

In West Virginia, an area which basically was pro-Union, there was bitter reaction after the war when ex-Confederates came into their state wearing the hated C.S. uniform. Those so doing were the West Virginians who had served in the C.S. Army, and, as in all border areas, the feeling was high. The governor of West Virginia complained to Secretary of War Stanton that the "loyal people of his State resented the insolence of these ex-rebels who still insisted on wearing their Confederate uniform.

7

Supply, Allowance, and Issue of Uniforms

SUPPLY OF UNIFORMS AND CLOTHING

In the early months of the war the Federal Government was unable to furnish all its new regiments with uniforms and clothing.

During the fall of 1861, the Federal Government purchased $800,000 worth of uniforms abroad. This led to strong resentment from home manufacturers and contractors. And this at a time when sentinels in Washington walked their beat in the snow clad only in their underwear, with no trousers nor overcoats! "Shoddy" became a household word during the war because of the large quantities of uniforms and clothing which were made of such inferior material as to fall to pieces in a few weeks after issue.

Unfortunately, this bad situation was aggravated by soldiers who often lost items of uniforms in excellent condition, threw them away deliberately, or traded them for tobacco or whiskey.

When the men did not leave their extra clothing by the roadside, they often destroyed such clothing to prevent any further use by civilians or enemy soldiers. For example, on arrival at Brandy Station, the 2nd Pennsylvania Heary Artillery unpacked their "bureaus" (the nickname for knapsack), and set fire to the contents. For each soldier, this involved burning up a government blanket, overcoat, dress coat, two or three "dog hair" shirts, short stockings, boots, shoes, and such miscellaneous items as playing cards and writing material.

Negro civilians who followed both armies as servants, cooks, teamsters, and laborers often wore discarded articles of uniforms. When the Confederate general Pettigrew's Negro cook was captured at Kinston, North Carolina, he was wearing a Federal dress coat. In explanation he told his Federal captors: "I took it from one of your dead during the Peninsular Campaign, and was allowed to wear it if I would turn the buttons with the eagles' heads down." And, as a soldier of the 27th Massachusetts Infantry expressed it: "Sure enough, *every eagle drooped.*"

A potent cause of loss of clothing was the pesky vermin which "inhabited" the men during long periods of campaigning when the men had no opportunity to bathe or wash their clothing. One of the first things the men did when leaving the front lines was to draw complete sets of uniforms and clothing and then build huge bonfires to burn up their old coats, pants, vests, shirts, socks, shoes, caps. If there were a few articles of clothing

Light artillery private, full dress. (Courtesy
The Smithsonian Institution)

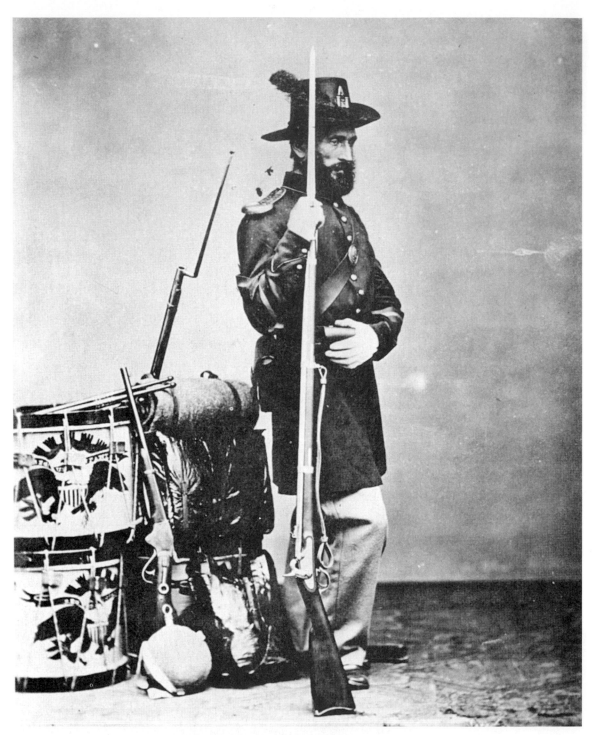

Engineers corporal, full dress, holding a
rifle, and beside him a field pack, canteen,
Sharps carbine, and two drums. (Courtesy
The Smithsonian Institution)

Cavalry sergeant, full dress. (Courtesy The
Smithsonian Institution)

that escaped, because they were too good to be burned up, these were at once cleaned and purified by a grease-extracting and vermin-killing souse and boil in hot soap suds.

Despite this waste, the Quartermaster's Department continued to expand its supply of uniforms. By mid-1862 the Department had purchased:

    1,281,522 overcoats
    1,446,811 uniform coats
    3,039,286 trousers
    3,446,520 boots and shoes

Before long the supply was ahead of distribution. In August 1862, the Federal Quartermaster General reported on hand some 600,-000 each of coats, trousers, underwear, and pairs of stockings. At the same time there were more than 500,000 pairs of shoes in stock. Yet soldiers in the field at this time too often were poorly clothed and without shoes. As the war progressed, there was an ever-increasing flow of uniforms and clothing from the main Quartermaster depots located at New York, St. Louis, Alton (Illinois), and Cincinnati and Steubenville, Ohio. The clothing made from 1864 to the end of the war was of excellent quality. It was strong and durable and was of local manufacture.

Coats were made by the Quartermaster Department at New York, Philadelphia, Cincinnati, and St. Louis; trousers were made at Quincy, Massachusetts. These Government installations, however, made only a fraction of the uniforms used by the Federals. Most of the uniforms and clothing was made by contractors at widely dispersed points in the North. By the fall of 1863, the Federal Army was fairly well supplied. Nevertheless, in that year, the Federals bought over 3,000,000 pairs of trousers, nearly 5,000,000 flannel shirts and drawers, and some 7,000,000 pairs of stockings.

Many women made uniforms for the soldiers. Soldiers' Aid Societies were organized to make uniforms and knit socks. Of course

large consignments of clothing were sent the soldiers as gifts from friends and relatives.

A benefit of local supply was that the provision of such clothing gave work to many communities. For example, the Michigan regiments in 1861 were clothed mainly by garments made in Detroit, thus "affording employment to hundreds of poor women" in that city.

In addition to Government contracts and local sources, uniforms were also imported from overseas. In August 1861, the Quartermaster's Department purchased 10,000 uniforms from France. These were of excellent quality. However, most uniforms were American-made, although throughout the war, many volunteers were poorly supplied in certain areas due to poor distribution.

The Regular Army was fairly well taken care of, but often the volunteers were uniformed by the states. Many militia regiments wore their peace-time uniforms to the front.

Specifications for uniforms and clothing were drawn up by the Quartermaster General's Office in Washington, D.C. Delivery was made to general depots under the control of the Quartermaster's Department. The depot quartermasters contracted with clothing manufacturers in their areas. Uniforms were drawn by army and department quartermasters for the units in their respective commands. Direct issue to the troops was made by the regimental quartermaster.

During the first days of the organization of a regiment, the busiest man was the quarter master. Not only did he have to issue all the equipment, he also was responsible for clothing the men. The quartermaster was assisted by the orderly sergeant who assembled the men for their clothing issue. The sergeants handed out overcoats as the men stepped up, with no reference to the size of the individual. It was up to the men to fit themselves the best they could by trading with one another. It really made little difference for there was not much "fit" to them

Infantry sergeant, full dress. (Courtesy The
Smithsonian Institution)

Soldier in fatigue coat. (Courtesy The Smithsonian Institution)

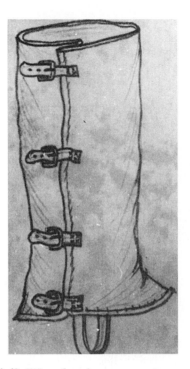

Civil War leggings or gaiters. (Courtesy
James Shutt)

Civil War shirt. (Courtesy James Shutt)

147

Civil War shoes. (Courtesy Francis A. Lord)

anyway. After the fat had exchanged with the lean, there were still some extra small or large sizes which the unfortunate few had to wear. Some soldiers cut the cape off because they saw no use to it; others cut the length down by a crude amputation with a pocket knife.

Soldiers normally had to repair their own uniforms or draw new ones. In some regiments repairs were done voluntarily by soldiers who were paid for such work by their comrades. There were no assigned shoemakers or tailors in the tables of organization for Federal units.

Each soldier was allowed a stipulated number of various clothing items per year. If a balance was due him at the end of a year, this balance was added to his allowance for the next year. If he had overdrawn on his

clothing allowance, he paid the difference to the paymaster at the mustering for pay at the end of the month. Ordinarily, clothing was drawn and issued twice a year, and at other times when necessary in special cases.

On the whole, the Federal Army was well uniformed during most of the war. For example, when Sherman completed his "march to the sea," his army of 100,000 men was completely re-outfitted in clothing. There were so many uniforms made by the North that large quantities were sold to the second-hand clothing dealers for years after the war.

UNIFORM ALLOWANCE AND ISSUE

Each Federal soldier was allowed by regulations the following yearly uniform and

Foot artillery sergeant, full dress. (Courtesy
The Smithsonian Institution)

Artillery musician, full dress. (Courtesy
The Smithsonian Institution)

Cavalry corporal, full dress. (Courtesy The
Smithsonian Institution)

Catlett's Station, Virginia, August 1862.
The station with U.S. military boxcars and
soldiers (Orange and Alexandria R.R.)
Photo by T. H. O'Sullivan. (Courtesy Library of Congress)

clothing allowance during his first five years of service:

YEARLY ALLOWANCE OF
CLOTHING FOR A

FIVE-YEAR PERIOD	1	2	3	4	5	Total
Hat with trimmings complete	1	1	1	1	1	5
Forage cap	1	1	1	1	1	5
Coat	2	1	2	1	2	8
Trousers	3	2	3	2	3	13
Shirt	3	3	3	3	3	15
Drawers	3	2	2	2	2	11
Bootees, Pairs of (Jefferson)	4	4	4	4	4	20
Stockings, Pairs of	4	4	4	4	4	20
Leather Stock	1	—	1	—	—	2
Great coat	1	—	—	—	—	1
Flannel sack coat	2	2	2	2	2	10

The Confederate uniform and clothing allowance, copied from the United States pre-1861 regulations was as follows:

ITEM	1st Yr.	2nd Yr.	3rd Yr.	Price
Cap	2	1	1	$ 2.00
Jackets	2	1	1	12.00
Trousers	3	2	2	9.00
Shirts	3	3	3	3.00
Drawers	3	2	2	3.00
Shoes	4	4	4	6.00
Socks	4	4	4	1.00
Leather Stock	1			.25
Overcoat	1			25.00
Stable Frock (Mounted Men)	1	1	1	2.00
Fatigue Overalls (Engineers, Ordnance)	1		1	3.00

As of December 8, 1862, the list generally followed in most units was as follows:

Cap, cover, jacket, trousers, shirt, drawers, shoes, socks, leather stock, overcoat, stable frock (for mounted men), fatigue overalls (for engineers and ordnance), blanket.

The regulations always specified the number of each item of the above which a soldier was allowed. If a balance was due him at the end of the year in his clothing allowance; he was paid that amount when his unit mustered for pay. If he had drawn items whose value exceeded his clothing allowance for the year, this amount was deducted from his pay.

Ordinarily, the company commander procured and issued clothing for his men twice a year. At other times in special cases such articles as the soldier might need would be issued to him. Each soldier's clothing account was kept by the company commander in a company book.

The following descriptive list of a private of the Second (German) Ohio Infantry was written by his company commander (Captain Th. Wich).

William Tubbee, Co. "K" was born in Hanover, Germanie, He is 33 (thirty-thry) old, and 5 feets 8 inches high, and was been in this rigiment from the forst day of commance. He god too sesters in the city of Toledo, Ohio.
William Tubbee received from his compaigne—

1. 1 blanket
2. 1 hat
3. 1 poar ov shies
4. 1 coat
5. 1 poar of pontoloons
6. 1 poar of pretches
7. 2 poar unterschirts
8. 2 poars stockens
9. 1 plaid
10. 1 naif
11. 1 forc.
12. 1 tinn cop

His hear is bron, noss is long, mouth is general, eyes are gray, moustache is lick his hear [like his hair].

Appendix A

Wagons of men of the U.S. Military Telegraph Construction Corps, Brandy Station, Va., February 1864. (Courtesy Library of Congress)

Raymond, A.   New York, N.Y.
Supplied uniforms under contract to C.S. prisoners.

Richardson, Spence, and Thompson   New York, N.Y.
Sold items to Federal officers, including some of general rank.
Specialized in insignia and uniforms.

Samson, A. C.   New York, N.Y.
Supplied socks under contract to C.S. prisoners.

Schuyler, Hartley, Graham and Co.   New York, N.Y.
Insignia and uniforms.

Scovill Manufacturing Co.   Waterbury, Conn.
Buttons.

Shipley, Roane & Co.   Baltimore, Md.
Supplied coats and pants under contract to C.S. prisoners.

Slater, John   New York, N.Y.
Military boots and shoes.

Smith, W. H.   Brooklyn, N.Y.
Belt buckles.

Sumner, George A.   New York, N.Y.
Supplied socks under contract to C.S. prisoners.

Talcott, James   New York, N.Y.

Supplied socks under contract to C.S. prisoners.

Tomes, Melvain & Co.   New York, N.Y. Army and Navy uniforms.

Walcott, J. B.   Boston, Mass. Supplied shoes under contract to C.S. prisoners.

Walker, Noah and Co.   Baltimore, Md. Supplied jackets and pants under contract to C.S. prisoners.

Warnock and Co.   New York, N.Y. Military headgear.

Waterbury Button Co.   Boston and New York Buttons.

Weinschenk, S.   New York, N.Y. Supplied drawers under contract to C.S. prisoners.

Wilkinson   Springfield, Mass. Belt buckles.

Wilson, Henry Crossed sabers.

Wilson, J. H.   Philadelphia, Pa. Buttons.

UNIFORM ITEMS

ALBRIGHT, CHARLES, Mauch Chunk, Pa.   100,000 pairs of bootees.

ARNOLD, MARTIN, AND POTTER Bootees.

ARNOUX, ANTHONY, 531 Broadway, New York, N.Y.   Overcoats, pants, jackets. Shared in contract for 15,000 Army uniforms for New York, May 27, 1861.

BALDWIN, F. B.   Uniforms, overcoats.

BANISTER, J. A., Newark, N.J.   Bootees.

BARNUM, CHARLES, New York, N.Y. Uniforms, overcoats.

BATCHELLER, E. & A. H. AND CO.   Cavalry boots.

BAYLAN, JAMES B.   Infantry trousers, blouses, cavalry jackets, artillery uniform coats.

BEINHEIMER, ADOLPH   Cavalry jackets.

BELLOWS, MARTIN, Philadelphia, Pa. 5,000 bootees.

BICTA, JOSEPH   Bootees.

BIGELOW, CHAS. D., 54 Vesey St., New York, N.Y.   Bootees, shirts, socks.

BLANCHARD, LEONARD, East Abington, Mass.   4,000 bootees, cavalry boots.

BROOKS, E. A., New York, N.Y.   Uniforms, overcoats, bootees.

BROWNER, H. H., Syracuse, N.Y.   50,000 bootees.

BRYANT, GEO. (or Seth?), East Bridgewater, Mass.   7,000 bootees.

BURKERT AND KOEDEL, Philadelphia, Pa.   10,000 bootees.

BUTTON, WORTHINGTON B.   Infantry trousers; cavalry trousers, overcoats, jackets; artillery uniform coats; Invalid Corps jackets.

CAHILL, S., New York, N.Y.   1,000 bootees.

CANFIELD, M. B. & SON, Orange, N.J. Bootees.

CHILD, PRATT AND FOX, St. Louis, Mo. Cavalry boots, many items of Army supplies.

CHURCHILL, L. AND H., Rochester, N.Y. 5,000 bootees.

CLAFIN, WILLIAM   Cavalry boots.

CLARK, AMOS   Greatcoats, cavalry jackets.

CLARK, EZRA, JR., New York, N.Y.   5,000 bootees.

CLOUD, STEPHEN, JR., Pa.   1,000 bootees.

COBB, HENRY, Boston, Mass.   12,000 cavalry boots.

COLBURN, C. AND CO., Boston, Mass. Cavalry boots, bootees.

COMSTOCK, J .S. & CO., St. Louis, Mo. Boots, shoes.

COOK, BENJ. F.   Negro brogans.

CORN, SAM'L, 59 Broadway, New York, N.Y.   Army clothing.

COTRALL, J. G. & SON, Albany, N.Y. Uniforms and caps.

COUGHLAN, LANGLEY, BOICE & CO., 34 Cortlandt, New York, N.Y.   Army clothing.

CUMMING, ALEXANDER, New York, N.Y.   75,000 bootees.

DEERING, WILLIAM   Cavalry trousers, canton flannel drawers.

DEVELIN, HUDSON & CO., New York, N.Y.   Overcoats, uniforms. Made uniforms for "Mozart Regiment" (40th N.Y. Inf.).

DEXTER, J. D., New York, N.Y. Bootees.

DICKERMAN, L. & CO., Philadelphia, Pa. Bootees.

DIXON, WILLIAM T. AND BRO. Negro brogans.

DOUGLASS, M. B., Newark, N.J. Bootees.

DOWNS, H. S., Boston, Mass. Bootees, cavalry boots.

ENDERS, WILLIAM F. & CO., Boston, Mass. Uniforms.

ENOS, D. C., Philadelphia, Pa. 100,000 bootees.

EVERS, JOHN A., Philadelphia, Pa. 25,-000 bootees.

FENTON, E. P. AND CO., Syracuse, N.Y. Bootees.

FOSTER, H. L. Cavalry jackets.

FOX, CHARLES, 62 Broadway, New York, N.Y. Caps.

FOX, E. W. 30,000 Army overcoats.

GARTHWAITE, J. C. Artillery and infantry uniform coats, blouses.

GEISSENDORFF, J. W. & CO., Indianapolis, Ind. Army clothing.

GILMORE, C., Raynham, Mass. Shoes for Mass.

GLASSER & BROS. Uniforms.

GODFREY, B. D., Guilford, Mass. Boots, shoes.

GOLDEN & DUNLOP, 522 Broadway, New York, N.Y. Caps.

GOLDSTEIN, B., 164 Broadway, New York, N.Y. Army clothing.

GOULD, THOMAS R., Boston, Mass. Bootees.

GRAY, W. H., Philadelphia, Pa. Patent for epaulettes, Nov. 12, 1861.

GREEN, Sharpless, Pa. Bootees.

GREEN AND BRO., St. Louis, Mo. Shoes.

HABER, ISAAC & CO. Infantry uniform coats and overcoats; artillery uniform coats; cavalry jackets and trousers.

HALL, BENEDICT & CO., New York, N.Y. Thousands of bootees, shoes.

HALL, SOUTHWICK & CO. Negro brogans.

HALLOWELL, CHARLES, Philadelphia, Pa. Bootees.

HALLOWELL, RICHARD P., Boston, Mass. Shoes, socks, underwear.

HANFORD, JOHN E., Brooklyn, N.Y. Contracted July 12, 1861 for: 40,000 sky-blue overcoats, 50,000 dark-blue infantry coats, 60,000 dark-blue pantaloons, 80,000 dark-blue sack coats, 100,000 pairs flannel drawers, 100,000 white cotton shirts.

HAZEL & CO., Philadelphia, Pa. Bootees.

HEIDELBACH, WERTHEIMER & CO. Uniforms.

HELLERMAN, WILLIAM T., Philadelphia, Pa. Bootees.

HENSELL, H. W. Sergeants' worsted sashes.

HORSTMAN BROTHERS & ALLIEN Infantry and artillery cords and tassels.

HOW, JOHN Uniforms, many varied items of army equipment.

HOWES, HYATT & CO., New York, N.Y. Bootees.

HUGHES, SAMUEL, Pa. Bootees.

HUNT, HOLBROOK AND BARBER, Hartford, Conn. Bootees.

HYATT, STEPHEN, New York, N.Y. Shoes.

JENKINS, LANE & SONS Bootees.

JOHNS, WILLIAM B., Georgetown, D.C. Patent for military cloak, Oct. 22, 1861.

JONES, AARON Stockings.

JONES, F. & N., Philadelphia, Pa. Shoes, bootees.

JONES, FREDERICK & CO., Boston, Mass. Negro brogans, bootees, cavalry boots.

JONES, WILLIAM H. Stockings.

KELLOGG, P. V. & CO., Utica, N.Y. Uniforms.

KELLOGG, PALMER P. Uniforms, overcoats.

KIMBALL, ROBINSON & CO., Boston, Mass. Cavalry boots, bootees, shoes for Co. "F" 15th Mass. Inf.

KING, D. R. & CO., Philadelphia, Pa. Bootees.

KOHNER AND BRO. Infantry overcoats.

KOLLINSKY, COLOMANNUS (et. al.), Washington, D.C. Patent for cap, Nov. 5, 1861.

LAMB, JAMES S. Uniforms.

LEE, JOSEPH Stable frocks, canton flannel drawers, chevrons, cavalry trousers.

Uniforms of Regular Confederate troops.

LEVICK, RASIN & CO., Philadelphia, Pa. Cavalry boots, bootees.

LEWIS, JOHN W., 44 Warren St., New York, N.Y. Shirts, drawers.

LIVINGSTON, BELL & CO., St. Louis, Mo. Uniforms, boots, canteens, knapsacks, Army clothing.

LONGSTREET, BRADFORD & CO. Army clothing.

LUDLOW, W. A. & J. C. Blouses.

MACK AND BROS., Cincinnati, O. Uniforms.

MANSFIELD, L. W. Knit shirts.

MARBLE, F. M., New Haven, Conn. Bootees.

MARTIN, JOHN T. Cavalry greatcoats and trousers; infantry greatcoats and trousers; artillery frock coats.

MARTIN, L. T. Infantry and cavalry trousers, blouses.

McCOMB, H. S. Bootees, leather neck stocks.

McDONALD, J. H., Albany, N.Y. Uniforms, caps.

McDOUGALL, FENTON & CO., Syracuse, N.Y. Shirts, socks.

McREA, WILLIAM H., Philadelphia, Pa. Bootees.

MEGARY, MICHAEL, Wilmington, Dela. Bootees.

MERRIAM, HENRY W. Bootees.

MERRIAM, S. S., New York, N.Y. Bootees.

METZGER, CHARLES Cavalry hat cords and tassels.

MOORE, ROBERT, Carlisle, Pa. Bootees.

MOYER, SAMUEL D., Norristown, Pa. Bootees.

MULDOON, WILLIAM, Philadelphia, Pa. Bootees.

MUNDELL, JOHN, Philadelphia, Pa. Bootees.

MURPHY, W. J. & CO., Philadelphia, Pa. Bootees.

MURPHY & CHILDS, 50 Dey St., New York, N.Y. Caps.

MURPHY AND GRISWOLD Forage caps, hats, trimmings.

OWENS, CHARLES H., Philadelphia, Pa. Bootees.

PARRISH, JAMES, 323 Canal St., New York, N.Y. Sold "French flannel Army shirts."

PASCAL, C. L., Philadelphia, Pa. Patent for military hat, Dec. 10, 1861.

PHILLIPS, L. J. AND I. Forage caps.

PIERCE BROS. & CO., Boston, Mass. Shirts, drawers, socks.

QUINN, HUGH Stockings.

RANSON, W. A. & CO., New York, N.Y. Bootees.

READ, HAMILTON & CO., Newark, N.J. 10,000 bootees.

REED, NAHUM Boots.

ROBINSON, JOHN P., Brookfield and Marlboro, Mass., and Dover, N.Y. Shoes.

ROEDEL, JACOB, Lebanon, Pa. Bootees.

ROSE, ALVIN Flannel shirts, overcoats, canton flannel drawers.

ROSS, ALLEN, Sing Sing, N.Y. Cavalry boots, bootees.

ROTHSTEIN, H., 140 Broadway, New York, N.Y. Caps.

SAXONVILLE MILLS Infantry overcoats.

SEAMLESS CLOTHING MANF. CO., 255 Canal St., New York, N.Y. Seamless overcoats for the Army and Navy.

SEARS, ZENAS, Boston, Mass. Bootees.

SELIGMAN, WM. AND CO., New York, N.Y. Uniforms, overcoats.

SHELDON, F. S. Uniforms.

SHELDON, J. L., Auburn, N.Y. Caps.

SHETHAR AND NICHOLS. Uniform hats.

SLADE AND COLBY. Flannel drawers.

SMITH, J. S., New York, N.Y. Patent for shoulder straps, June 18, 1861.

SMITH AND RICE. Infantry trousers.

SNYDER & CO., Philadelphia, Pa. Felt hats.

SOUTHWICK, HENRY C., Albany, N.Y. Socks.

Uniforms of Confederate troops.

STADLER & BROS., Cincinnati, O. Uniforms, Army clothing.
STEWART, ALEX T. Shirts, socks.
STRONG, ALEX, New York, N.Y. Bootees.
STRONG BROS. & CO., Albany, N.Y. Socks, shirts, drawers.
TALCOTT, JAMES. Stockings.
TAYLOR, JAMES, Baltimore, Md. Bootees.
TEMPLE, D. & W. Bootees.
TERHUNE, JOHN, Newark, N.J. Bootees.
TERRY, JOHN R., 397 Broadway, New York, N.Y. Caps.
TRASK, A., New York, N.Y. Bootees.
TROUNSTINE, A & J & CO. Uniforms.
TYLER, MOSES (MORRIS?), New Haven, Conn. Bootees.
VAN SICKLER & FORBY, Albany, N.Y. Uniforms, socks, shirts, drawers.
WARE, PRESTONE, Newton, Mass. Bootees.
WARE AND TAYLOR, Boston, Mass. Bootees.
WEBSTER AND CO. Bootees.
WEISS, F. W., Mount Vernon, N.Y. Patent for military cloak, Dec. 10, 1861.
WHEELER, CHARLES B. Bootees.
WHIPPLE, J. F., New York, N.Y. Patent for cap, July 16, 1861.
WHITNEY, JOSEPH & CO. Negro brogans.
WHITTMORE & CO., St. Louis, Mo. Felt hats.
WICKES & STRONG. Uniforms.
WOLVERTON, G. A. & CO., Albany, N.Y. Uniforms, shoes.
WOOD, WILLARD & PRENTICE. Socks, shirts.

CONFEDERATE STATES

Bailey, Thomas R. & Son, Charlottesville, Va. Shoes
Baldwin, H. E. & Co., New Orleans, La. Buttons
Bellenot and Ulrich, New Orleans, La. Louisiana State buttons
Bents, J. A. and S., Baltimore, Md. Buttons

Bird, Wm. and Co., London, England Buttons
Bouis, S. and Co., Richmond, Va. Belt buckles
Buckeye Land Factory, Charlottesville, Va. Cloth for uniforms
Buckley, S. and Co., Birmingham, England Buttons
Cadman (?), Columbus, Ga. Buttons
Campbell, S. Isaacs & Co., London, England Buttons
Canfield and Brothers, Baltimore, Md. Maryland buttons
Chatwin and Son, Birmingham, England Buttons
Courtney and Tennent, Charleston, S.C. Buttons
Crenshaw Mills, Richmond, Va. Woolen uniform cloth
Dowler, W., Birmingham, England Buttons
Eagle Manufacturing Co., Columbus, Ga. Cloth for uniforms
Firmin and Sons, London, England Buttons
G. & Cie (Gourdin & Co.), Paris, France Buttons
Gibbes, James G., Columbia, S.C. Uniforms, hats, boots, shoes
Gminder, Jacob, Baltimore, Md. Buttons
Godchaux, Leon, New Orleans, La. Louisiana State buttons
Halfmann, E., Montgomery, Ala. Buttons
Halfmann and Taylor, Montgomery, Ala. Buttons
Hammond, Turner and Bates, Manchester, England Buttons
Hammond, Turner and Sons, Birmingham, England Buttons
Herbert and Co., London, England Buttons
Hoppe, F. A. & T., Charlottesville, Va. Boots and shoes
Howie, J. M., Charlotte, N.C. Buckles
Hyde and Goodrich, New Orleans, La. Buttons
Jamestown Woolen Mill, Old Jamestown, N.C. Cloth for uniforms
Jennens and Co., London, England Buttons
Kent, Paine and Co., Richmond, Va. Buttons

Lavasseur, H., New Orleans, La. Buttons

Leech, John and Co., Madison County, Va. Boots and shoes

Lewis, E. M. and Co., Richmond, Va. Buttons

Loyd, W. S., Columbus, Ga. Military caps

Micon, B. H., Tallassee, Ala. Uniform cloth

Mitchell and Tyler, Richmond, Va. Buttons

Munds and Henning, Columbia, S.C. Shoes

Myers, S. A., Richmond, Va. Virginia and North Carolina buttons

Remsen, C. P., Columbia, S.C. Military hats

Rothchild, S., Columbus, Ga. Uniforms

Rouyer, C., New Orleans, La. Buttons

Rowyer and Lavasseur, New Orleans, La. Buttons

Rush, S., Forestville, Va. Hats

Sappington and Co., Columbus, Ga. Shoes

Silver, R. W. and Co., London, England Buttons

Smith and Wright, Birmingham, England Buttons

Starkey, Jos., London, England Buttons

Steele and Company, Charleston, S.C. Hats

Stradtman, Frederick Wm., Cahaba, Ala. Shoes

Tait, P., Limerick Buttons

Terry and Juden Co., New Orleans, La. Louisiana State buttons

Thorn, Saul D., Columbus, Ga. Buttons and caps

T. W. and W. (Trelon, Weldon and Weil), Paris, France, Buttons

Van Wart Sons and Co. Buttons

C. and J. W. (C. and J. Weldon), London, England Buttons

Wendlinger, C., Richmond, Va. Virginia Buttons (possibly post-Civil War)

Wildt, W., Richmond, Va. Buttons

Wilt and Klinc, Columbia, S.C. Buttons

(Uniforms of Confederate troops (Virginia, Maryland, South Carolina, etc.)

161

FEDERAL PATENTS FOR UNIFORM ITEMS

(The following list is for the entire war period—1861 to 1865. Items such as shoes and boots, where no specific military use is indicated in the patent description, are excluded.)

DATE	ITEM	PATENTEE	PATENT NUMBER
1861			
July 16	Military cap	J. F. Whipple	32,849
Nov. 5	Military fatigue cap	C. Kollinsky, et. al.	33,651
Dec. 10	Military hat	C. L. Pascal	33,900
Nov. 12	Epaulettes	W. H. Gray	33,702
Nov. 19	Overcoat and tent, convertible	Henry J. Phillips	33,752
Oct. 8	Overcoat, tent, and knapsack	Joseph Short, 2nd	33,468
1862			
Aug. 26	Army and Navy caps	W. F. Warburton	36,315
Feb. 25	Military hats	W. F. Warburton	34,538
1863			
Aug. 25	Military caps	S. Massman	39,667
		(Patent antedated July 20, 1862)	
1864			
	None		
1865			
	None		

CONFEDERATE PATENTS FOR UNIFORM ITEMS

Category	Patentee	Patent No.	Date
Wooden-soled shoes	E. S. Collins Aspinwall, Va.	130	Dec. 30, 1862
Wooden-bottom shoes	G. M. Rhodes and A. Bingham Talladega, Ala.	68	Feb. 1, 1862
Wooden-soled shoes	Sylvester L. Burford Lynchburg, Va.	171	May 21, 1863
Wooden-soled shoes	Robert Creugbaur Austin, Texas	167	May 1, 1863
Wooden-soled shoes	Robert Creugbaur Austin, Texas	195	Aug. 23, 1863
Half wooden-soled shoes	Robert Creugbaur Austin, Texas	196	Aug. 28, 1863
Wooden shoe sole	A. F. Purejoy Forrestville, N.C.	264	Nov. 22, 1864
Military cap	Henry Domler Wilmington, N.C.	56	Dec. 14, 1861

Appendix B

SMITHSONIAN INSTITUTION PRESERVATION OF FLAGS AND MILITARY UNIFORMS

Identify Fibers

Without knowing the material a flag or military uniform is made of and/or its degree of deterioration, it is difficult to give advice on the exact technique to recommend for its preservation because fibers differ in their reactions to various methods of preservation. All fibers, including sewing thread and trim as well as the ground fabric, have to be identified. Each individual flag and uniform has its own characteristics which also must be taken into careful consideration before any preservation work is done. However, there are some general methods that have been used which will give some idea of the problems involved. After the materials incorporated into the object have been identified and its condition has been carefully recorded, the owner must decide which, if any, of the following suggestions would best suit his article.

Experienced Personnel

It is most important at this time to emphasize the necessity of having highly specialized personnel do the work. This is not the type of work that one can enter into blindly, but it takes experience in knowing which technique is best for the individual item, and then more experience in handling the actual flag or uniform without harming the fabric. Sometimes it is to the good of the old item to do nothing at all, lest an uncertain hand do more harm than it has already suffered.

It is also necessary to have the proper equipment available.

Clean

Before a flag or uniform is prepared for exhibition or storage it should be clean. Dirt contains abrasive particles that act almost like a razor between the yarn and damage the fibers if the article is moved. The condition of the object in question is a guide as to how this dust may be removed. If the object is in fairly sturdy condition—in other words, if it does not powder to the touch or yarns break when being handled—then loose grit and dust can be removed safely by covering the fabric on a flat surface with a fiberglass screen and gently going over the covered object with a low-suction hand vacuum cleaner.

Testing the dyes carefully is especially important in flags since the ones that have been exposed to the elements have much soiled fibers that may resist penetration by detergents during an abbreviated period of contact. Too short a test will therefore fail to reveal dyes that bleed.

Besides the mechanical danger that abrasive dirt may break fibers, there are some chemical dangers. Cotton or linen, which decay in continuous acid state; silk or wool, unhealthy in the alkaline state; or iron-containing rust stains continuing to oxidize with accompanying weakening of the fabric are all examples of such chemical dangers which can be removed if the fabric is washed and neutralized.

Dyes need to be tested in every case before a treatment with any solution. Rust may be removed by sponging the area with a solution

A fire Zouave relating his experience of the Battle of Bull Run in the street at Washington.

of one tablespoon of oxalic acid in one cup of warm water (i.e. about 6% by weight). N.B. Oxalic acid is POISONOUS. Rinse this out thoroughly and then continue with a cleaning process. Undesirably acid fabric can be neutralized by an alkaline bath (most detergents are alkaline), and an undesirable alkaline state is neutralized by a weak acid, for example acetic or white vinegar. The acidity or alkalinity of solutions can be tested by litmus paper. If a pH meter is available, that is the best means of accurately recording acidity or alkalinity.

Some museums recommend "dry cleaning" or what is sometimes referred to as "chemical cleaning" for wool or silk. It has been observed to date that the objects that have been dry cleaned have a dry "hand" (feel)—either because the process has removed some moisture or because loss of natural oils has taken place. If only moisture has been lost it will be recovered naturally during the following days. Modern dry cleaning plants have large machines designed to do the most cleaning in the least time without special precautions against mechanical damage. As far as we know, no dry cleaning facility has a separate museum section for special handling of fragile textiles. It is not altogether unfeasible to think of dry cleaning textiles in a museum but the proper handling, equipment, ventilation of room, and adequate rinsing so that old soil is not redeposited would all have to be carefully worked out. We never press any uniform or flag with an iron. This is harmful if old dirt is pressed in and it can dry the fibers.

Fumigation and Insecticides

When wool or starched cotton uniforms or wool flags are given to the Smithsonian Museum they are put into fumigation chamber at once. (In 1968 a new vacuum fumigation chamber was put into operation, using a diluted ethylene oxide gas as the fumigant.) After three weeks the uniforms or flags are returned to the present fumigation chamber and run through a second time. From this second fumigation the articles are placed in storage units. They lie flat. Paradichlorobenzene or naphthalene is put into containers in these units to protect the fabrics continuously, but in no case do insecticides touch the fabric. Do not use plastic containers for these insecticides because the container will become soft. If the uniform has to be hung on hangers use only wood hangers; as plastic hangers would soften and bleed, if colored, under the constant insecticide exposure. Naphthalene is used when leather, patent leather, or visors are present because paradichlorobenzene has a deteriorating effect on these materials. Naphthalene too deteriorates leather, but in small quantities to a lesser degree than paradichlorobenzene. A decision

has to be made sometimes to establish which is more important; the wool or the leather. If the wool is more important then it has to be protected by the least harmful insecticide.

Units are checked frequently and the insecticides are checked and replenished every six months. Every six weeks, a lindane spray is painted in six-inch strips on the floor across the storage entrance door, around the storage unit bases, and in between the storage units. This precaution checks any insects which may enter after the initial fumigation.

A full discussion of insect and microorganism damage to textiles and what controls to use can be found in a paper delivered at the 1964 IIC Delft Conference on The Conservation of Textiles by H. J. Hueck entitled, "Biodeterioration of Textiles and Its Preventions" from the International Institute for

Recruiting group for colored regiments.
(Courtesy Chicago Historical Society)

Conservation, c/o The National Gallery, Trafalgar Square, London, W.C.2.

There is a "home" method of fumigating which uses thymol vapor. A full explanation of this system can be found in *The Conservation of Antiquities and Works of Art* by H. J. Plenderleith, Oxford University Press, 1956.

Storage

The preferred storage for flags and uniforms is for them to be laid flat in one-layer thickness. This gives full support to the whole article without having any strain on any one part. They should be in storage units which are dustproof. Again, the ideal would be for the flags and uniforms to be laid out flat on a surface which would glide in and out on rollers from the storage units so the textile

would not be handled any more than would be necessary.

The fibers in fabric react to temperature and humidity change, changing their dimensions and rubbing against one another, so this should be avoided. A temperature of 68°F. and relative humidity of not over 50% should be kept as constant as possible. These conditions can be measured by means of a thermometer and hair-hygrometer, respectively. The optimum of 50% humidity is stated because it was found in a study which Mr. Hueck records (reference previously sited) that there can be as much as a 20% fluctuation in humidity in one room. Fungus growth is almost nonexistent under 70% humidity, so to be safe subtract the 20% fluctuation possibility and you find great safety in a 50% relative humidity standard. To stop

Prayer in Stonewall Jackson's camp. Etching, 1862. (Courtesy Library of Congress)

Father T. Quinn, 1st R.I. Light Artillery.
(Courtesy Library of Congress)

insects from growth takes even a lower humidity. Lower temperature retards insect attack better. The ideal temperature for storage areas would be 50°F., but this is generally too cool for general use.

Fabrics should not be in airtight cabinets. Fabrics need to "breathe" for continued life. Dust can be kept out with filters, but air should be allowed to circulate.

SMITHSONIAN INSTITUTION NEEDLEWORK PRESERVATION OF MILITARY UNIFORMS

Many uniforms have suffered varying degrees of damage through the years from hard wear or insect attack. To prevent further deterioration, the damaged sections of the uniforms are reinforced.

If the ground fabric is in good condition, having only a few small holes or tears, it can be restored to a more presentable appearance by stitching a similar piece of cloth under the damaged portions. This new fabric should be as close in yarn, weave, texture, weight, and color to the original ground fabric as possible. It can be dyed to obtain the best possible match in color. The yarns are then matched up warp to warp, and the old fabric is mended down to the new fabric. This type of restoration is not only desirable for the appearance of the garment, but is also necessary to stop any further tearing of the cloth around the damaged portion.

If the entire garment is badly worn, having a weak ground, and many holes and tears, it may be necessary to line it completely with muslin after patching the holes as described above. This new lining should be stitched at such intervals necessary to minimize the weight of any large portion of the original fabric on itself.

Some coats have metallic fasteners on the shoulders to secure the epaulettes and these have become weak from supporting the epaulettes for a long period. Several layers of muslin the width and length of the shoulder are placed inside to reduce any strain on the points where the fasteners are stitched to the ground.

Collars and cuffs which usually received the hardest wear sometimes are so deteriorated that the facing is in shreds. Lining the inside of these portions with muslin and covering the outside with crepeline is the restoration technique used. This sheer fabric can be dyed to blend with the cloth it covers. Another area that frequently deteriorates rapidly on uniform coats is the lining that holds various forms of chest and shoulder padding in place. Here again the use of crepeline will keep the padding in place and assist in preventing further deterioration.

Crepeline has also been used to reinforce early silk waist coats. Here a muslin lining was placed inside the entire garment and crepeline, dyed to match the color of the cloth, was then stitched through the original fabric to the new lining.

Bibliography

OFFICIAL PUBLICATIONS

United States
*Official Records of the Union and Confed-
erate Armies in the War of the Rebellio i.*
128 vols. and atlas. Washington, 1880-19(1.
*Official Records of the Union and Conf ed-
erate Navies in the War of the Rebell on.*
31 vols. Washington, 1894-1927.
General Orders, War Department. 1861- ,865.
General Orders, Army of the Cumbe land,
1862-1865.
General Orders, Army of the Potomac 1861-
1865.
General Orders, Army of the Te nnessee,
1864.
*Regulations for the Uniform and Dress of
the Army of the United States J ine 1851,*
(William A. Horstman and Sons), Phila-
delphia, 1851.
*Regulations for the Uniform and Dress of the
Army of the United States 1861.* Wash-
ington, 1861.
*Revised Regulations for the Army of the
United States 1863,* Washington, 1863.
*Illustrated Catalogue of Arms and Military
Goods,* (Schuyler, Hartley and Graham)
New York, 1864.
*Regulations for Uniform and Dress of the
Navy of the United States* (March 8, 1852).
*Regulations for the Uniform and Dress of
the Navy of the United States* (January
28, 1864) Schuyler, Hartley and Graham,
New York.
*Regulations for the Government of the
United States Navy,* Washington, 1865.
*Regulations for the Uniform and Dress of
the Marine Corps of the United States,
October 1859.* Philadelphia, 1859.
*General Regulations for the Military Forces
of N. Y.,* Albany, 1863.
Case, Theo. S. *The Quartermaster's Guide,*
St. Louis, 1865.

Confederate States
General Orders, War Department, 1861-1865.
*Regulations for the Army of the Confederate
States,* Richmond, 1863.
*Uniform and Dress of the Army of the Con-
federate States.* Richmond, 1861.
*The Militia and Patrol Laws of South Caro-
lina to December 1859.* Columbia, S.C.
1860.

Newspapers and Periodicals
Army and Navy Journal, 1863-1865.
Boston Transcript, 1861.
Century Magazine, January 1889.
Charleston *Courier,* April 1862.
Charleston *Daily Courier,* 1860-1861.
Charleston *Evening News,* May 1861.
Frank Leslie's Illustrated Newspaper, 1861-
1865.
Harper's New Monthly Magazine, 1860-1865.
Harper's Weekly, 1861-1865.
Journal—Company of Military Historians,
1949-1967.
Mobile *Tribune,* October 1862.
Our Living and Our Dead. Raleigh, 1874-
1876.
*Personal Narratives of Events in the War of
the Rebellion* (Papers of Rhode Island

Soldiers and Sailors Historical Society) 6 Series, Providence, 1878-1905.

Richmond *Daily Dispatch*, 1860-1861.

Rochester in the Civil War (Rochester Historical Society) Publications XXII, 1944.

Southern Bivouac, Louisville, 1882-1887.

Southern Historical Society Papers. Richmond, 1876-1900.

The Bivouac ("An independent military monthly") 3 vols. 1883-1885.

The Confederate Veteran. Nashville, 1893-1932.

The Land We Love. Charlotte, 1866-1869.

Books

[Anonymous]

History of the Fifty-Seventh Regiment Pennsylvania Veteran Volunteer Infantry. Meadville, Pa.

History of the Twenty Third Pennsylvania Volunteer Infantry. N.P. 1903.

History of the Ram Fleet and the Mississippi Marine Brigade. St. Louis, 1907.

Under the Maltese Cross (155th Pennsylvania Infantry) Pittsburgh, 1910.

Albert, Alphaeus H. *Buttons of the Confederacy*. Hightstown, N.J., 1963.

Allan, William. *The Army of Northern Virginia* in 1862. Boston, 1892.

Barnard, George S. *War Talks of Confederate Veterans*. Petersburg, Va. 1892.

Bigelow, John Jr. *The Campaign of Chancellorsville*, New Haven, 1910.

Boyle, John Richards. *Soldiers True* (111th Pennsylvania Infantry) New York, 1903.

Brainard, Mary Genevie Green, *Campaigns of the One Hundred and Forty-Sixth Regiment New York State Volunteers*, New York, 1915.

Buffum, Francis H. *A Memorial of the Great Rebellion* (14th New Hampshire Infantry) Boston, 1882.

Clark, Walter (ed.) *Histories of the Several Regiments and Battalions from North Carolina in the Great War 1861-65*. 5 vols. Raleigh, 1901.

Collins, Geo. K. *Memoirs of the 149th N.Y. Vol Inft*. Syracuse, 1891.

Dana, Charles A. *Recollections of the Civil War*. New York, 1898.

Davis, Charles E. Jr. *Three Years in the Army* 13th Massachusetts Infantry) Boston, 1894.

DeChanal, General. *The American Army in the War of Secession*. Leavenworth, Kansas. 1894.

De Leon, T. C. *Four Years in Rebel Capitals*. Mobile, 1890.

Eggleston, George Cary. *A Rebel's Recollections*. New York, 1875.

Eldredge, D. *The Third New Hampshire (Infantry)*, Boston, 1893.

Emmons, Clark. *History of the Seventh Regiment of New York*. 2 vols. New York, 1890.

Evans, Clement A. *A Confederate Military History*. 13 vols. Atlanta, 1899.

Floyd, Fred C. *History of the Fortieth (Mozart) Regiment New York Volunteers*. Boston, 1909.

Gerrish, Theodore, and Hutchinson, John S. *The Blue and the Gray*. Portland, Maine, 1883.

Grant, U. S. *Personal Memoirs*, 2 vols. New York, 1886.

Grayson, A. J. *"The Spirit of 1861"*—History of the Sixth Indiana Regiment, Madison, Ind., 1875.

Haynes, Martin A. *A History of the Second Regiment New Hampshire Volunteer Infantry* . . . Lakeport, N.H., 1896.

Hopkins, Luther. *Bull Run to Appomattox*. Baltimore, 1908.

Johnson, David F. *Uniform Buttons*. 2 vols. Watkins Glen, N.Y., 1948.

Kemper, C.W.H. *The Seventh Regiment Indiana Volunteers*. Muncie, Ind., 1903.

Lewis, Waverly P. *U. S. Military Headgear 1770-1880*. N.P. 1960.

Lincoln, William S. *Life with the Thirty-Fourth Mass. Infantry*. . . Worcester, 1879.

Lord, Francis A.
They Fought for the Union, Harrisburg, Pa. 1960.
Civil War Collector's Encyclopedia, Harrisburg, 1963.
Bands and Drummer Boys of the Civil War, New York, 1966.

Lusk, William Thompson, *War Letters*. New York, 1911.

McCarthy, Carlton, *Detailed Minutiae of Soldier Life in the Army of Northern Virginia*.

Richmond, 1882.

Miller, Francis Trevelyan (editor) *The Photographic History of the Civil War.* 10 vols. New York, 1911.

Moore, Frank B. (Editor) *The Rebellion Record.* 12 vols. New York, 1861-1868.

Nash, Eugene A., *A History of the Forty-fourth Regiment New York Volunteer Infantry.* Chicago, 1911.

Plum, William R., *The Military Telegraph during the Civil War in the United States.* 2 vols. Chicago, 1882.

Rauch, William H., *History of the "Bucktails"* Philadelphia, 1906.

Rauscher, Frank, *Music on the March 1862-65.* Philadelphia, 1892.

Roe, Alfred S. *The Fifth Regiment Massachusetts Volunteer Infantry.* Boston, 1911. *The Tenth Regiment Massachusetts Volunteer Infantry.* Springfield, Mass. 1909.

Russell, William Howard *My Diary North and South.* Boston, 1863.

Spicer, William A., *History of the Ninth and Tenth Regiments Rhode Island Volunteers.* Providence, 1892.

Smith, Daniel P., *Company K, First Alabama Regiment,* Prattville, Alabama, 1885.

Stevens, C. A., *Berdan's United States Sharpshooters in the Army of the Potomac.* St. Paul, Minnesota, 1892.

Stiles, Robert, *Four Years under Marse Robert,* New York, 1903.

Thompson, Gilbert, *The Engineer Battalion in the Civil War,* Washington, D.C., 1910.

Thompson, S. M. *Thirteenth Regiment of New Hampshire Volunteer Infantry,* Boston, 1888.

Tilney. Robert, *My Life in the Army,* Philadelphia, 1912.

Vail, Enos B. *Reminiscences of a Boy in the Civil War,* Brooklyn, N.Y., 1915.

Van Alstyne, Lawrence, *Diary of an Enlisted Man.* New York, 1910.

Vautier, John D., *History of the 88th Pennsylvania Volunteers . . . 1861-1865.* Philadelphia, 1894.

Wallace, Lew. *An Autobiography.* 2 vols. New York, 1906.

Ware E. F., *The Lyon Campaign in Missouri,* Topeka, Kansas, 1907.

Wiley, Bell Irwin. *The Life of Johnny Reb,* Indianapolis, 1943.

Wilhelm, Thomas. *A Military Dictionary and Gazetteer,* Philadelphia, 1881.

Wilson, Joseph T., *The Black Phalanx,* Springfield, Mass. 1888.

Wingate, George W., *A History of the Twenty-Second Regiment.* New York, 1896.

Wise, John S., *The End of an Era.* New York, 1899.

Index